Storyteller

Irish Myths, Legends, and Folktales for Americans

Juilene Osborne-McKnight

Illustrated by Mara Kate McKnight

PELICAN PUBLISHING

NEW ORLEANS

The word "Pelican" and the depiction of a pelican are trademarks of Arcadia Publishing Company Inc. and are registered in the U.S. Patent and Trademark Office.

ISBN 9781455627998

All photographs by author unless otherwise indicated

Printed in the United States of America
Published by Pelican Publishing
New Orleans, LA
www.pelicanpub.com

Contents

Acknowledgments

First thanks go to my former student, now my colleague, Professor Robert Johnson (Theology) who repeatedly exhorted me to write this book. Theologians are good at exhortation.

I am also grateful to our dear friend Eoin (Owen) Flynn of Co. Waterford, who helps me with things Irish on every book and who always makes me laugh. *Go raibh maith agat mo chara.*

Gratitude, always, to my husband Tom, who makes straight the crooked path, who seems to believe that I hung the moon and though I did not, his belief in me is balm in Gilead.

Gratitude to my daughter Mara, who did these delightful illustrations while working in retail management during a Christmas season. Proof that still there are miracles.

Authors always say that we are grateful to our publishing companies, but in this case, I truly mean that. My long-time, recently-retired editor Nina Kooij was the quintessential professional, and I now take delight in my fellow storyteller/editor Justin Mason. Pelican Publishing has been a delight to work with through both books.

I am a storyteller, so I want to thank the storytellers who have taught with me and told with me throughout the world. I owe a tremendous debt of gratitude to tellers from the Native American nations, in particular Joseph Bruchac (Abenaki), Eileen Charbonneau (Shoshone/Huron/Metis/Irish), and the Jemison/Lay family (Seneca/Haudenosaunee) who hosted us so many times for festivals. I also want to thank Fr. Andrew Greeley, gone now to *Tir-nan-Og,* for his book advice, his life advice, his Irish stories, and for being the Irish grain of sand in the Catholic Church oyster. A most important thanks to our mom and dad, who filled every day from dinnertime to bedtime with stories, music, books.

I will always be grateful to DeSales University, where I am Professor Emerita, for giving all of my books and stories fertile soil for growth.

Please Tell Me a Story:
Some Opening Considerations

The modern Irish place high value on "good craic"—the magic that occurs when everyone is together in a room, singing, telling stories, binding the room in laughter and delight. Stories are alive—not in some vague philosophical sense, nor in the sense of muscle and bone.

Photo of the author telling stories in Ireland by Diana Florence Koch. Reprinted with permission

Stories have breath, life, and longevity. In fact, our ancient Celtic ancestors knew that an oral story—a story that is told—has agency.

When I was learning to be a storyteller, I studied with many masters of the form, but my honored teacher, Joseph Bruchac of the Abenaki Nation, gave me the best advice I ever received: "Never memorize a story," he said. "Just carry it and let it tell itself."

A story will read a room. This surprises me every time. It will look out at the crowd, and it will know what that crowd requires on that night for that story to enter their consciousness, to speak right to their spirit. And the story will tell itself that way.

This might sound woo-woo, but ask any writer and they will tell you the same thing; there comes a moment in the writing of a novel when the story takes over, when the writer can close his or her eyes and just take dictation for a while. How can this be?

Carl Jung called it the "collective unconscious" of the human race. Neuroscientists will tell you that story has developed as an evolutionary mechanism to aid our survival. We will discuss both of these further in our "Legends" section.

What our Celtic ancestors knew was that the stories must be preserved against all things—against time, against wars, against death. For thousands of years, they did that through bardic training. Writing was forbidden in the ancient Celtic world because they believed that power resided in the story and to write it down would thin its power. Consequently, young men and women trained for twelve years to memorize the stories, to carry them from place to place in a combination of prose and poetry that was recited by the firesides of every rath in Ireland.

Later, after the waves of invasions began in Ireland, the monks knew that in order to preserve the stories, they would *have* to be written down, copied, carefully protected, and hidden from invaders. They knew that the stories would be lost forever if they did not preserve them, as would Irish, the language of the tales.

Consider this: a culture's stories contain everything that culture is—what they value, what they fear, their sense of humor, the dance and patterns of their language, their attitudes toward war, toward hospitality, toward marriage, toward children, toward the gods, toward the sacred earth upon which they live. If the stories die, all of that dies with them.

So, our monks hunched over their scriptorium tables by daylight or by the spitting light of tallow fat candles. When they were not copying the gospels or the psalms, they rendered thousands of years of oral stories onto vellum. More surprising still, they did this in the vernacular—in Irish—the origin language of our ancestors. We would have no myths of the ancient gods of Ireland, no legends of our great heroes were it not for the medieval monks, who had Vikings and Normans and British invaders breathing down their necks for hundreds of years. We should think of this as a stunning act of nationalism and bravery, because it was.

For the folklore of Ireland, we owe thanks to the Anglo-Irish founders of the Celtic Revival and to the ethnographic folklorists who preserved those stories. Collectors went from town to town recording the folklore of the village people word for word, rendering, as closely as possible, their own beautiful idiom and pronunciation. Then, writers like Yeats and Lady Gregory assembled and edited these collections. So, we still have stories of leprechauns and pookahs, fairies and ghosts. But even more than that, we still have the people who told them, in all their linguistic, cultural, and spiritual glory. Just watch the play *Riders to the Sea* once to understand what would have been lost if JM Synge had not gone to the Aran Islands.

Our own Stephen King says that a book is a conversation across time, even across death, between writer and reader. That is certainly so. When you read a book, even if the author is long-gone, you are in direct contact with that writer. The book is alive, as is the author. Of course, King would have been right at home in the pantheon of Irish writers alongside Sheridan le Fanu, Bram Stoker, and our brilliant Oscar Wilde with his portrait in the attic.

Stories are a kind of portrait in the attic, aren't they? They remain vital, generation after generation. They tell us who we are and who we were. Of course, there are dozens of collections of Irish myths, legends, and folktales, but what they lack, for our American purposes, is context.

Context is one thing I strove to provide here, for American readers who might not know the full Irish story. Where is this story set geographically? Can I show you a picture? A map? When is this story set historically? Can I give you a sense of that time and place, of the beliefs and attitudes of the time? Can I clearly divide myths from legends from folktales so that we can understand what differentiates these categories?

I also hope that you enjoy my retellings. I deliberately chose retellings here, rather than translations from the Irish or exact transcriptions from nineteenth century Irish tellers. I wanted these stories to come alive for you, with action and dialogue, with shifting voices, clear conflicts and sensory settings. Literal translation and transcription, while beautiful and lyrical, might not allow you to enter the story, in the same way that, as speakers of American English, it takes us some time to adjust ourselves to Chaucer or *Beowulf* or Shakespeare. I wanted you to be able to drop right into the story, to see/hear/taste/touch/smell our ancestors and their wild, magical world.

All of this storytelling is enhanced by the whimsical and beautiful art of my daughter, so much of it reflective of the art of our ancestors, whose braidwork indicated a firm belief that there is no death.

The death of storytelling must worry us these days. As a professor, I can tell you that we are living in strange academic times, in which a collective of "stemwits" have decided that everything that makes us human—art, history, music, dance, philosophy, literature, theater—no longer qualifies for collegiate study, because art takes time. As a result, humanities majors are vanishing from American universities at a headlong pace. Behind that, of course, lurks the specter of AI.

Our ancestors knew the importance of stories and art. They knew that we live on in story, that story connects us to everything human, to every human who preceded us and every human who will follow. They knew that human art is a connection to the divine.

Imagine, then, a monk in the chill stone of his monastery, dipping his quill into the ink, positioning the vellum, knowing that he is about to speak to you, here, in the twenty-first century. For a moment, he intones the words that give him endurance, courage—and the certainty that the work is necessary, is sacred: *In the beginning was the Word…*

Oh yes. Exactly that important.

Bail, O Dhia, ar an obair.
Bless, O God, the work.

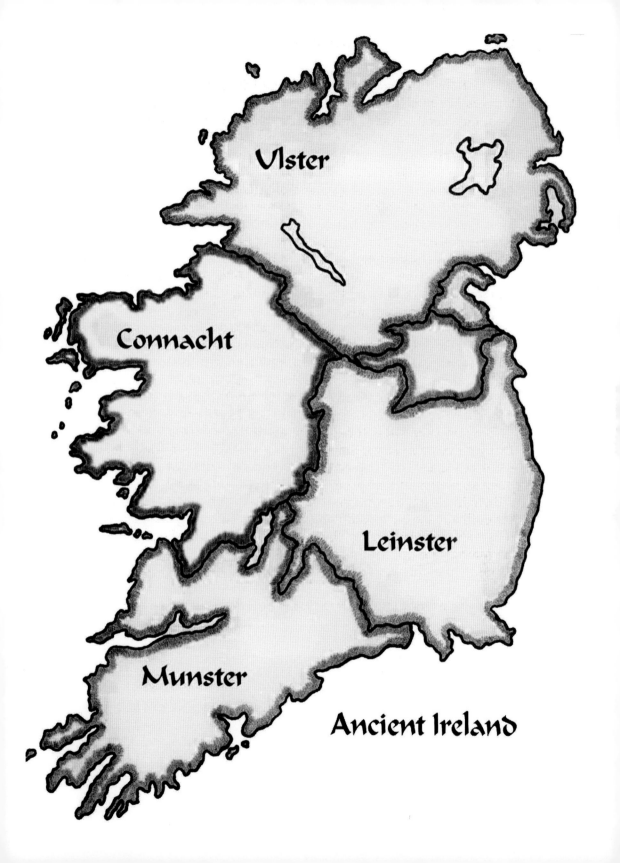

PART I
Myths
How Did We Get Here and Why

Part I: Myths: How Did We Get Here and Why

Chapter 1

Myths of the Tuatha de Danaan of Ireland

Dark Eyes and the Saving of Lugh

I was a tribute child, yes. That is what they called us, those Nemedians who birthed us and gave us away.

Of course, they had no choice; we were part of the tribute demanded.

We have also heard, here on this forsaken rock, that some of the mothers and fathers could not give up their children—crops, yes, surely, and even cattle—but they could not accede to the demands of the Fomorians. We have heard that those parents planned and prepared before the Samhain cull, escaping to the east, then making the dangerous crossing to the continent in the round coracles of fishermen.

I will choose to believe that this is true, that there were those for whom their children were more important than all else, even death.

I am not one of those children.

My parents turned me over to the Fomorians with no more than a blink or a look back. It was a Fomor woman who named me, Eithne, daughter of Balor One Eye. She called me Súile Dorcha. It means Dark Eyes.

In all my life, she was the only person who was kind to me. And so, when the time came, I saved her child. This is the way of the wheel.

I learned many things early. I learned that most of the Fomor women are barren; in truth this is a blessing of the gods, as the Fomor men are piratical—self-absorbed and warlike. Because many of the Fomor women are barren, those who take in tribute children sometimes love them as if they were their own.

The Fomor men do not seem to realize that we who are their slaves will one day outnumber them. This will be well. This world needs no more Fomor.

The exception, of course, is Eithne, the woman I serve. She too has suffered at the hands of her father. You will know the prophecy, surely. All of us do. Long ago, a druid prophesied that Balor would be killed by his own grandson. So, he locked poor Eithne in a tower by the sea and gave her many serving women, but no contact with any man.

The only man she had ever seen was her hideous, one-eyed father.

But I was the foil for Balor's greed. Oh, you will hear that it was Birog the druidess who cast the spell that saved the child, but all of it was less magical than that.

I will tell you the tale.

Balor had heard of the magical cow called Glas Gaibheann and he determined to steal it from Cian of Eire. But Cian is of the De Danaan. Even we Nemed, who have no quarrel with the Tuatha, know better than to trouble the magical people. But Balor thought to trouble them.

Foolish One-Eye. There are things far more powerful than his glistening, unveiled eye. When he brought the cow here to Tory Island, Cian, whose name means long endurance, followed. He was son of Dian Cecht, Physician of the Others, and Cian bore powerful magic in his own right.

You will know what happened. It is what always happens to the greedy ones. Birog, the druidess, brought Cian here. Brought him to this tower. Brought him, surely, so that the prophecy could be fulfilled. He climbed the many stairs, and when he saw our beautiful Eithne and when she saw, for the first time, a man other than her one-eyed father . . . well, you know the ending. Surely, you do.

We hid her pregnancy. All of us. Her serving women. All of us Nemed. All of us hoped that the prophecy would be fulfilled.

But her father, Balor, came to visit her when she was birthing those boys. Triplets. A threesome of hope.

And he threw his own three grandsons into the wild and heaving sea.

I hid when I heard him coming. He had begun to notice me by then, I in my twelfth year. So I hid.

And when I knew the shameful thing that he had done, it was I who clambered down the rocks, I who found the one boy who had been washed up on the shore, I who protected him and stilled his cries and sent for Birog the druidess. When she came on a still and moonless night, it was I who put him in the coracle and watched her row away.

I have told my mistress; the knowing gives her hope.

I do not know what will become of the boy, but Birog will see to it that he is well hidden.

Eithne has named him Lugh.

For a long time, I expected to die for my transgression. I expected that Balor would learn of what I had done, would lift the cloak from the terrible eye, would turn it in my direction. But I had held that boy against me for three days and three nights, and I was willing to die.

Balor is a being more terrifying than any of the Fomor on this rock.

On the main island they believe him to be a monster, a god, a machine of war. And it is true that his eye is most formidable. But he cannot open the eye alone. He needs the help of we who serve.

Here is the secret of Balor One Eye. He is a man. A very large man, yes, perhaps eight feet tall, gone to fat from too much drink, too much food, too much of everything. Hair grows down the length of his back, along his forearms, covering his massive chest, long enough on his chin that he can braid the length and sometimes has us do that for him, while he hums and sways and feeds on haunch of deer. But still, he is just a man. His body works like the body of every man. Yes, he carries his club wherever he goes, a bat three times the length and width of a normal hurling stick. So that gives the main islanders pause. More than anything else, they fear the eye.

As do we all. Even the creatures of the forest fear the eye.

Despite the eye, Balor is still a man. That means he could be defeated. By the right champion.

As of yet, that one has not appeared.

And the eye, I will say that it is formidable, though he needs us to open it, a feat we accomplish with long sticks, wrapped with cloth and soaked in warm water. The eye sits, always closed, in the center of his forehead. Bit by bit we open the eye. Little inch by little inch. And when it is open, it kills. Yes, kills. I have seen the eye bring down a huge buck. A wolf. I have seen it bring down the enemies of the Fomor. Lightning shoots from it. Heat and fire. Balor One Eye is just a man, as I have said.

But for the terrible eye.

I would wager my two eyes against his one. Because I have the Farsight. Some of us do, we Nemed. We can see far, far out to sea, over the water. On a good day, on a day of no sea mist, I can see the mainland, see the fires from the mainland, see the smoke floating up from the villages.

And so it came to be that, staring out to the east, from high in the tower window, I saw the little coracle approach. And I knew that it came for me. I told my Lady Eithne. She cut my hair then, like the hair of a boy. She dressed me in rough clothing, procured for me a sailor's cap.

"Dorcha beag," she whispered to me. "Little Dark One. Go to my child. Protect him with your life. Tell him there will come a day when the king of the Tuatha de Danaan will require his help."

And so, I climbed my way down the rocks, sat still in the coracle of the druid, then found my way to the blacksmith who was raising the boy. He does not know. He thinks me a young boy still; he is surprised by my love for the wee baby. He will never know that I keep my mistress safe with my silence, that I watch the boy with my far-seeing eyes.

But the boy will know the truth when I tell him.

Our golden Lugh.

Our hope.

Who Are the Little People and How Did They Come to Ireland?

Three myths explain how the Tuatha de Danaan came to Ireland. All three agree on when they arrived on Beltaine—the first of May.

- Myth one has them arriving from Greece in Greek biremes.
- Myth two says that they were the people who escaped from the explosion of the volcano that sank the magical city of Atlantis. Therefore, they are Atlanteans, which might explain their long lives and their magic.
- Myth three says that they arrived from the sky in triangular cloud ships. Shades of Ancient Aliens.

But none of these myths addresses the rich strangeness of who they were . . . and are.

The little people are known as the Tuatha de Danaan, the people of the goddess Danu. They are often called the "Little People," the "Others," the "Sidhe," (pronounced shee). They are *not* leprechauns, who belong to the folk tradition of Ireland. The Others are much more dangerous. They are beautiful, nearly five feet tall, and they radiate blue or golden light. They do not grow old, and they rarely die. When they do die, they simply go to Tir-nan-Og, an isle in the western sea, where they feast, tell stories, and listen to music until they are ready to return. Then they reincarnate.

They are powerful in battle, knowledgeable in medicine, have powers to heal and powers to harm, strong powers to bewitch and confuse. Among their members are those who will intermarry with humans, protect humans, and love them. But also among their members are those who possess terrible dark powers and who live to exercise those powers against humans, as you will see in the stories of this section.

Perhaps most notable regarding their interactions with humans, the Little People seem to live in a dimension in which time moves much more slowly than does human time. Numerous stories tell of humans who go into the world of the sidhe, convinced that they have been with the little people for three days, only to return to their own place and time to discover that three hundred years have passed and that all of their friends and family are long gone. You will read one such foundational story in our "Legends" section.

The First Battle of Mag Tuired

The hand was the work of craftsmen. This we all knew. Silver, chased with spirals, hammered with hounds and hearts. Our smiths had made sure that it was a thing of stunning beauty.

Each finger had its own purpose. Lightning. Streams of fog. One finger coaxed music from the air.

Our physicians had made sure that the glove functioned better than a hand, that the impulses of Nuada's arm could move the hand, articulate the fingers.

We had even given our king a name that would honor the hand and his sacrifice: Nuada Argetlamh. Nuada Silver Hand.

But it was not enough. We were trapped by our own laws. The law that a king must be unblemished. The law that his sword hand must be strong.

Oh yes, we had defeated the Firbolg, ceded to them their bogs in Connacht, sent them to the wild edge of the Western Sea, where they no longer troubled us. We had allowed Sreng, their chief, to live, he who had cut off the hand of our king, this at the behest of our good king.

Oh, why did they challenge us to war? Did they not know what we were, from whence we came? We had no desire to displace them. They were poor and slow, these little dwellers of the bog, always carrying their bags of fertile soil about the rocky country. We would not have displaced them. They would rarely have seen us, for we manage time in ways that they could never know. But no, they wished for us to leave the green isle. We who had nowhere else to go, whose island had exploded into the swirling maelstrom of the sea.

In the end, they cost us our king.

Members of the council wept when the decision was announced. A new king was to be named—a man who was whole in all his parts.

But, we know now, a man who was not whole in his spirit.

Bres the Beautiful.

Bres, the son of Eri, one of our own, but fathered by Elatha, Prince of the Fomorians, the dark raiders of Túr Rí. Had we forgotten what we knew of them? Had we forgotten their evil Balor of the one eye? Did we think that because he was fathered of a Tuatha woman, he would not carry the dark helix of his male line?

I am a physician, Airmid, daughter of the great physician Dian Cecht, sister of the brilliant geneticist Miach. What we know of medicine, of the helixes of Tuatha and human, we can never reveal. Such secrets would reveal our origin and our age. We know that the helixes of life move like a river in all beings, human and other.

Perhaps we had grown too secure in our knowledge, in our powers.

All of the Nemed had departed by that time, sailing for Greece, taking those of their children that they could rescue, leaving the rest behind. We no longer heard their Fomor tales and the raiders had been quiet for some time, perhaps reduced in numbers by their vanished serving people.

Or perhaps we chose Bres for his beauty. Great beauty sometimes allows for great evil.

Bres was a man of no generosity; he did not entertain visitors, did not feed them or lodge them. Hospitality is our most sacred law; he violated it. He was also a man of appetites; he longed for gold, for women, for cattle, and for praise. And in the end, he sold us out to get them.

Do you know the myth of Narcissus? Among our previous hosts, the Greeks, it was the most powerful of cautionary tales. Bres was the incarnation of that myth, a man so taken with himself, so certain that he deserved wealth and power and beauty that he could not believe that anyone would go against him.

And when we did, when we Tuatha de Danaan awoke and saw what we had elected, we began to move, secretly, to displace him.

That is when he betrayed us.

He gave the Fomor the secret codes to our gates, entrance to our cities beneath the surface of Eriu. He captured his own people as slaves, forcing the Tuatha de Danaan to serve the dreaded Fomor. Dagda, our great and generous statesman was forced to dig the trenches around the Fomor forts, those trenches designed to keep us out of the Fomor villages. He did this with nary a complaint; some days I could hear him singing as he dug, his song designed to boost our defeated spirits.

At last, Cairbre, our most honored poet, composed a satire against Bres. City to city he recited it, an act of such courage and bravery that none of us will ever forget it. Do you know the power of words? Do you know that they contain everything, everything, to make worlds and to right wrongs? Once that satire had been read from city to city, all tides turned against Bres. But how to defeat him? He had been elected king.

Secretly, and without the permission of our father, Miach and I began the work of recreating for Nuada a real arm, a human arm, an arm that would join to his stump sinew to sinew and nerve to nerve. Such work was forbidden, for that knowledge would have revealed us to the human world and terrified them, so that we would not be welcome anywhere.

But a despot must be defeated, by language or by science or by secrecy. Or all of these.

We did not know then how it would all unravel.

Or how we would be saved.

We had not yet met Lugh.

The River Cong in County Mayo, near where the First Battle of Mag Tuired takes place.

Lugh Samildánach

When the boy who called himself Samildánach arrived for the fourth time at the king's summer crannog, Amlaib tried hard to ignore him. By the gods, could the boyo be more irritating?

Samildánach, ha.

All Craftsman indeed.

He had shown up on the first day, claiming, of all things, that he was the finest horseman in all of Eire. Did he not know that their king was Nuada, who could ride standing?

"Give me a horse!" the boy had cried, his face upturned to Amlaib, who leaned against the window frame of the guard tower. "For the time is coming when the king will need my help."

At this, Amlaib laughed aloud.

"Give me the king's horse if you like, and I will show you," the boy insisted.

"The king's horse? Are you daft boy? No one rides the king's horse but the king."

But Barrfind, Amlaib's companion in the tower, had an idea that neither of them could resist. "Let's give him Manthrower. That will get rid of him for good."

Manthrower was the most vicious horse in the stables of any rath in Eire. He kicked and bucked. He bit, once permanently scarring one of the king's cohort by biting through the muscle of his cheek. Everyone called him the capall dubh, the black horse. So Amlaib had dispatched a laughing Barrfind, who returned with the kicking, head-whipping beast, barely in his control, and handed over the reins to the boy who called himself "All Craftsman."

At first, the horse reared up on his hind legs, spinning his mighty hooves in the air, but the boy stood to the side, holding the reins, the look on his face one of patient waiting. When the horse came back to earth, the boy reached into the pocket of his tunic and withdrew a carrot as if he had been carrying it in anticipation of just such an event. Manthrower drew back his lips and pinned his ears.

"Here we go," whispered Barrfind.

Amlaib leaned over the edge of the window frame in the guard tower.

"Well, boy?" he asked. "If you are indeed the All Craftsman as you claim, such a horse should be no trouble to you."

For answer, the boy stepped closer to the horse and blew out a long breath in the direction of the horse's twitching nose. The horse stood stock still.

The boy fed the horse the carrot and the horse took it like a lady at table. Then the boy stepped back slightly, leaped into the air and stood, one foot in front of the other, on the sleek black back of the mighty horse.

"Oh this will be good," said Barrfind.

But the horse stood absolutely still.

The boy, seeming to find his balance, lowered his arms. He made a soft noise, a kind of deep-throated clicking, and the mighty black horse launched into a perfect canter, the boy standing on his back as if it were the solid, unmoving earth. Around the lake they rode, with Barrfind and Amlaib moving from window to window in the guard tower to follow their progress. When at last they returned full circle, the boy simply slid to a seated position on the horse's back and looked up at the tower, his youthful face alight with delight.

"What say ye now?" he asked Amlaib. "Will ye take me to see the king? For he will need me soon."

"I will not," said Amlaib. "But you may take the horse, boy. No one will miss him here."

"I will return tomorrow," the boy said. He and the horse departed as one being.

Amlaib turned to Barrfind. "What did we just see there?" he asked.

"A haughty boy who is good with horses. Nothing more," said Barrfind.

But Amlaib found himself looking forward to the boy's return.

And return he did the very next morning, standing on the back of the great horse, his wool cloak billowing in the wind, his golden hair alight with sunlight.

"I am Lugh Samildánach," he called up to the tower. "I am come to serve the king."

Amlaib leaned against the window frame. Today he was alone in the tower, so he acknowledged what the boy had done. "Impressive feat with the horse, boy. But it does not make you good at all things. Only good with horses."

Lugh nodded.

A Crannog

An Irish crannog or lake fortress was an actual village or stronghold in the middle of a lake. It was entirely man-made. A ring of logs or upright posts were driven into the lake bed and filled in with gravel. On this base, huts and dwellings were built, as was a causeway and a guard tower. A small clan might live on a crannog or a chieftain might use it as a fortress.

"I thought that you might say that. But I am also good at smithy. Look!" He threw a silver object toward Amlaib, who caught it from the air. "This I made for you," the boy said.

Amlaib inspected the object. It was an arm torque, crafted of silver and chased with patterns of running hounds. Truly, it was an object of great beauty.

"Nothing here tells me that you made this," Amlaib called down. "Though it is fine work indeed. What village are you from?"

"A village where the smith has taught me his craft."

"That you would have to prove. I suspect that the smith has given you his craftwork to bring to this place."

"Bring me to your smith, and I will show you."

"I cannot leave my post."

"Good man. The king is lucky to have such a loyal one as you."

Amlaib narrowed his eyes.

"Do you think your flattery will tempt me to believe you?"

"I do not. But I am good as well at the silver tongue and sometimes the glib talk can turn or stop a war."

"We are not at war."

"Not now, no. But the dread Fomor bide their time, do they not?"

Amlaib had to give him that.

"True," he said. "The Fomor bide and raid, raid and bide."

"Your king might be helped by one with a glib tongue."

"And sure, you see yourself as that one, aye?"

"Aye," the boy nodded affably. He plucked an apple from his tunic and threw it up to Amlaib and then sat astride his horse, eating an apple of his own.

"I suppose you will tell me you also grew these apples," said Amlaib.

"Not at all," the boy replied. "But sure, they are delicious."

They ate for a time in companionable silence.

"I've renamed the horse, you know," the boy said at last. "Windrider. For together we are the wind itself."

Amlaib yawned. "You are that and I will not take it from you."

"You grow weary watching," said Lugh. "Here, I will play the singing music for you that you may regain your alertness." From the bag on his back the boy withdrew a small harp and ran his fingers over the strings. They made a mellifluous harmony. Then, with no hesitation, he began to pluck a merry tune from the strings.

From high in the tower, Amlaib listened and smiled. Truth be told, he had never heard a better harpist, even in the hall of the king. When the song finished, he called down to the boy, "In truth you are good at many things, boy. Who is your father and where is your rath?"

"Oh my father is a right, good man. He has made sure that I have been well-educated in all the crafts. If you believe me now, will you let me in to see the king? He will be needing me soon."

"I will not," said Amlaib. "For my job is to protect the king from all distractions and obligations while he is here at the crannog. He gets precious little time to be still, our king. And I will not interrupt him."

The boy spoke. "As good as I am as a harpist, I am as a poet. As good as I am riding my horse, I am at running. As good as I am at smithy, I am as wheelwright. As good as I am at sorcery, so I am at medicine. Your king will need all these skills. And too, I am a master swordsman. I can throw a spear farther than any man alive!"

"Do you know our champion, boy? Ogma Honey Mouth fights with us."

"Ah, the father of language he! Well, I revere him well, for, as I said, I am a talker. Bring him here and let us converse together."

But Amlaib knew his job. "I will not disturb him. He is in conference with the king. And as I've told you, we have men with all these skills."

"But do you have any who have them all in one?"

"No," Amlaib conceded. "We do not." At last, he felt he had to give the lad a chance. After all, he was indeed good at many, many things. He pointed to the high hut at the center of the water. "That is the king's hut," he said. "When my shift is complete, I will take you to him."

The boy took the last bite of his apple and threw the core into the forest.

"There is one more skill that I failed to tell you," he said, rising to his feet on the back of Windrider. "For I can swim underwater longer than any man alive. And I will swim to your king."

And with that, the boy executed a perfect arc into the water, slicing the surface without a splash.

By the time Amlaib climbed down from his tower and ran the long causeway to the king's hut, the boy was coming up from below the water, having swum the length of the lake without surfacing for a single breath.

Amlaib presented the boy to the king, telling him first about the horse and the harp and giving the king the exquisite silver torque.

King Nuada regarded the dripping swimmer before him. He stood, only to discover that the boy Lugh was more than twice his height.

"Who is your father?" the king demanded, "and from where your clan?"

"I am the son of Cian," said the boy, "grandson of Dian Cecht, the Physician, and Danu . . ."

"By the gods!" the king exclaimed. "We have heard the rumors. That you survived. Grandson of the Danu. But also the son of a Fomor woman."

The boy nodded. "I know my story. I am Lugh Samildánach. If you will have me, I will defend you, Nuada Argetlámh. And in your defense, I will earn yet another, yet a greater name."

Ogma, Ogmios

Known as the god of language, Ogma Honey Mouth is the brother of the Dagda. He was known as the inventor of the Ogham language that still decorates crossroad stones throughout Ireland. (Most scholars, however, date the Ogham language to the fourth century AD) Ogma was also known the originator of poetry and is often portrayed with gold chains coming from his mouth, symbolizing the power of language to bind us to people or principles.

An Ogham stone at an Irish crossroads

Ogham is a stick language that reads from bottom to top. Each grouping of sticks represents both a letter and a tree, with all the symbolism that tree holds. So, for example, the letter D or Dair would be represented by the symbol below. However, Dair also stands for the oak tree, the most sacred tree in Celtic religious practice. All religious ceremonies were held in oak groves, and the druids believed that the mighty oak trees with their upraised arms were always in an attitude of prayer. So venerated were the oak trees that the name alone meant wisdom.

D=Dair=Oak=Wisdom.

The crannog was transformed by darkness. Torches appeared upon the palisade and along the causeway. Their light shimmered in the water and shapes seemed to appear and disappear below the surface. At last, a mist arose off the lake, making the torches look smoky, obscuring the bottom half of the crannog and spinning itself like rivers across the field that ran to the trees. Mac Aidan stood.

"Now we may go."

"No! Not now!" Little Corra stood rooted, one hand clasping the trunk of a young sapling. "The water is the home of the sidhe and this fog is their breath. It will ensnare us in the darkness and we will be trapped with them in the place between the worlds."

Mac Aidan made an impatient sound and reached for Becan's bridle which was loosely secured to a branch. Aislinn stayed his hand.

"Do you not remember the terrors of your childhood?" she asked softly, indicating the pinched pale face of Corra in the starlight.

Aislinn knelt before Corra and stretched her hands out before her, seeking the little light that made them gleam. She drew Corra's hands into the light with her.

"You need not be afraid child, for you and I are like the sidhe."

Corra gasped. "How can this be? They are the Others."

"Long ago and longer, the Others lived like we do upon the land of Eire. They were called the de Danaan, the people of the goddess Dana and they were people of light and song. Then came the sons of Mil, the Milesians, with thirty ships to battle the De Danann. The De Danaan were afraid. They cast a fog upon the sea and hoped that the Milesians would lose their way, but they sailed around Eire three times, then came to land."

"And they killed the people—the De Danaan?"

"Nay child, for the old ones were wise. They sent the sons of Mil back to the sea and they raised a storm of magic power. Many of the ships disappeared. At last, the survivors came to shore and the Da Danaan were defeated."

"Did they die?"

"Not all of them. Those who lived disappeared into the mounds and the hills, beneath the waters where they still remain. Still others sailed away to Tir Nan Og, the land of youth where they live among the gods. Do you see why we need not fear them? We are like the De Danaan, you and I. We are cast away in Eire and those we love have gone to Tir Nan Og."

Corra nodded solemnly.

"I do see now. Can you speak to them priestess? Can you tell them not to fear us?"

Aislinn smiled.

"We will do this together, child."

Corra reached up for Eoghan's hand. He knelt beside them. Aislinn looked up in surprise at the watery silver tracks that lay along his cheeks. She gathered their hands together in the gleam of the moonlight, intoned her plea to the people of the sidhe.

"We who are mortal must pass.
Sing for us the song of the sidhe,
Light the dancing ring.
We will return at last, at last.
Now we who are mortal must pass."

She released their hands, stood, silent, holding her hands still in the light. Then she tipped back her head and issued out a sound, high like wind, half the cry of an animal, half the song of a human. She sustained her keening on a long breath against the darkness, down the field toward the crannog.

Mac Aidan swore beneath his breath. The hackles on Sheary's neck stood up and he began to howl in his peculiar wolfhound way. A small contingent of warriors still strapping on their arms and lighting their torches came streaming across the causeway and into the field at the edge of the water.

Thus, borne upon a Druid chant and the howl of a wolfhound, the little party entered the crannog of O'Domnhnaill.

The Second Battle of Mag Tuired

From all of our cities, deep beneath the earth, the Tuatha de Danaan came. Secretly, they came, each city bearing its most powerful weapon, its best provision.

Murias brought the very cauldron of the Dagda, food to feed an army on the march.

From Gorias, our smiths bore in the spear that they would give to Lugh, a spear they swore could not be defeated by any warrior who held it.

Nuada's sword, the thin blade polished and honed, was returned to him from Findias, for Nuada's hand had been restored, bone to bone, sinew to sinew. And now that he was fully human once again, he could fight the Fomor when they came.

From Falias our people came, secretly bearing the Lia Fail, the stone of kingship. For a new king must be crowned.

The author with the Lia Fail on the Hill of Tara. Supposedly brought to Ireland by the Tuatha de Danaan, the stone screams or sings when the true King of Ireland is crowned. In this photo, it is not singing. Photo by Thomas McKnight.

In the seven years of his reign, Bres the Beautiful had carried our proud people to ruin. He demanded tributes and more tributes—the grain from our fields, our best cattle, our children as slaves in the long tradition of his Fomor people. Our Dagda, father of our people, dug their trenches. Ogma, the poet, so weak and thin that we could see his bones, carried their firewood.

Know this, humans. Even the great Tuatha, even this most ancient and magical people can be subjugated by a despot. For under the rule of Eochaid Bres, Bres the Beautiful, not even a wisp of smoke from our chimneys went untaxed. To Bres, all of everything was his due. A people who are not free must rise.

Rise we did. By the hundreds and the thousands we converged on the Plains of Mag Tuired and all of us were ready to die for our freedom.

And many would die. So many in the sorrows of the telling.

Bres had gathered to him an army of Fomor, his father's people—though to give him credit, his own father, Elatha Mac Delbeith, refused to help his son, saying that such an unjust kingship had earned its own demise.

Balor of the One Eye had no such scruples. He came to the field of battle with an army of thousands, the numbers of the Fomor swelled by the warriors from the islands of the Hebrides, swelled further by the great ships of the Northmen, those we call the Lochlanders.

Even Balor's great eye was adorned by a ring that would allow his attendants to lift it, to turn it against all of the Tuatha de Danaan.

It did not matter that our druids had enchanted the battlefield. They had deprived the enemy army of water, they had caused earthquakes to tremble the earth beneath their feet, to topple the hills upon them. They had enchanted our own wells, so that if we were wounded, our warriors could enter the waters and be healed.

But none of it, none of it, could save our true king, Nuada.

How brave was Nuada. How fearless and how strong. He rode into battle astride his leaping stallion, his purple cloak swirling around him. But it took just one lift of the eye of Balor, just one turn of his head in the direction of Nuada to unseat our great king. The Fomor beheaded him. Beheaded the best and truest king the Tuatha de Danaan had ever known.

They held his head aloft and the wailing and weeping that issued forth from the field of battle could have torn the hearts of the Tuatha de Danaan.

Until Lugh rode into battle.

Oh they had held him back well enough, his foster fathers, the chieftains of Ireland. For they feared that they would lose him, wished to keep his skills in abeyance.

But Lugh had seen the death of Nuada, the king who had taken him in when he was just a boy.

So Lugh broke loose from them.

Standing tall on the back of Windrider, he rode into the midst of the fighting, lifting his great spear so high over his head that it caught the sunlight.

"Better death than bondage!" he called to the people of the Tuatha de Danaan. "For we are of Spirit and Wind. And as Spirit and Wind shall we fight."

And fight they did. Thousands died. Fomor and Lochlanders and Hebrideans. And thousands of our own, a race of people so old that we seldom died. But now we littered the battlefield.

"Come forth One Eye," Lugh called at last. "Come forth and see your grandson, he whom you threw into the sea."

And then the Fomorians brought Balor of the One Eye to the battlefield. They sat him on a great stone. They gathered up the long spears that would open the baleful eye. Slowly, slowly they lifted the lid. The old monster turned his eye in the direction of the voice, his grandson of the long-ago curse.

But our Lugh was prepared. Our Lugh Samildánach.

For he stood on the back of his horse as if both he and the horse were still. And from the pocket of his tunic, he drew out his slingshot and his stone. The great stone hurtled toward the eye, even as Balor turned the eye in the direction of his grandson.

But the aim of the stone was true.

The eye was driven deep into the back of the old monster's skull.

The tide of the battle turned at last.

Everywhere Lugh's spear flashed, a bolt of lightning, a shaft of sunlight, and then back into his hands, unblunted and glimmering, thanks to the rapid work of our smiths.

At last, the Fomor were defeated, banished off the coast for all of time. Balor of the One Eye was dead. They allowed Bres to live, our council, though many of us cannot see why. They set him to teaching the human skills of planting and harvesting, he who harvested selfishness and death.

We lost our beloved King Nuada, but Lugh had stood in his stead.

For his bravery on our behalf, our Lugh was given a new name, a

name that will hew to him for all of time. Lugh Lamhfada we called him. Lugh of the Long Arm, for the flashing prowess of his sunlit spear.

We regained our freedom.

At least until the humans came to our shore.

But that is a tale for a thousand years.

That is a tale for a long, looming day.

Carrowmore Burial Cairns, County Sligo

Many scholars think that the Second Battle of Mag Tuired took place near Lough Arrow where the neolithic passage graves of Carrowkeel dot the plains. Here, one of the passage graves of Carrowmore, near Lough Gill, gives a feel for the rich strangeness of these battles. For a fictionalized account of these battles, see my novel *Song of Ireland*.

Dusk was falling on the Plain of Mag Tuired.

In doorways between the standing stones, the Three Sisters waited. Opposite her, in separate doorways, Eriu could see Banba and Fodla. She had hoped to find Airmid in the city below, to supply each of her sisters with an arm, but the Ancient was nowhere to be found, applying herself to their own command to hide the arms, Eriu thought, securing them from Macha.

In each doorway of the circle, she could see Danu spear-carriers, one facing inward toward the circle, two facing outward toward the forest at the base of the hill.

They scanned the forest anxiously for their companions.

"They come," she whispered. "Danu, guide my hand."

No sooner had she spoken the words then the first dogs burst into the circle, running wildly in across the open space, criss-crossing each other. Eriu saw the outward-facing spear carriers turn inward toward the dogs momentarily, then return to post.

The inward carriers pointed their spears; arcs of blue light flashed across the open space. There was a high squealing sound from some of the dogs.

Now Danu spear carriers began to run in among their companions; they were flanked by the horses of the Danu. Eriu did not see Amergin among them but she cringed as one of the horses trampled over one of the Danu spear carriers. She saw him tumble beneath the horse's hooves, saw Metaphor slip from him as he fell.

"Physicians!" she called into the gathering dusk.

A flash of blue light sparked in an empty doorway. Two physicians swept onto the field and spirited the little Danu back between the uprights only to vanish below.

"By the gods!" cried the Milesian on horseback, the look on his face reflecting terror.

Then suddenly, the whole company was upon them, scrambling up the hill, dogs and horses, spear carriers and riders, Milesian runners, their swords clanging metal on metal. Flashes of blue light echoed crazily around the circle. Eriu heard screams but she could not tell if they were Danu or Milesians. It crossed her mind that creatures in pain screamed alike regardless of their origins.

Now flash after flash began to appear between the doorways as physicians came and went with the wounded.

Eriu heard the sound of hooves behind her; a horseman swept past. She stayed still and silent in her doorway, waiting for the signal to use the portals, to unleash upon the Milesians the full fury of the time portals.

Suddenly, she felt a huge hand at her throat and the cold horror of a thin metal blade against the soft flesh.

The voice of Amergin boomed out over the chaos.

"I have as prisoner Eriu of the Danu. Cease or I will kill her as she stands."

Chapter 2

Myths of Love and Loss

The Wooing of Etain

Midir, the king of the fairy folk, was rotund and red-bearded, full of laughter. The greatest joy of Midir's life was his wife Etain, the fairy queen. Etain was kind and beautiful. Her hair was the color of the copper leaves of autumn, her skin as white as the wings of swans. When Etain sang in her high, sweet voice, the fairy folk said her song rivaled the harps of heaven. Etain was beloved by all, all that is but Femnach.

Femnach, the witch woman, hated Etain. She hated her voice and her beauty. More than anything else Femnach hated the goodness of Etain's soul.

One day, Femnach heard the sweet sound of Etain's singing. Concealing herself deep within her dark cloak, Femnach followed Etain into the forest.

Etain waded into a little stream. She stood in a shaft of sunlight, singing a happy song. To Femnach, Etain looked like a magical bird. Her gown of purple silk was shot through with weavings of red and silver and gold. Her blue and green cloak was fastened at the shoulder with a brooch of gold. Femnach could no longer bear Etain's beauty or the sweet magic of her song. Suddenly, she had a wicked idea. Femnach raised her hands and cast a spell.

> *"Etain become a creature of the air.*
> *Fly far from Midir,*
> *Fly far from Eire.*
> *No song for comfort,*
> *No rest from care."*

Femnach watched, hoping that Etain would become an ugly, black

crow with its rasping caw. But even under the spell of
Femnach's evil, Etain's beauty shone through. Before
Femnach's eyes, Etain was transformed as a beautiful
butterfly. Her blue and green wings shimmered with
markings of purple and red, silver and gold. Nor could
Femnach take away Etain's lovely voice, for when Etain
flapped her butterfly wings, they made a humming
sound sweeter than the harps of heaven.

Now Femnach was terrified.

"The people of the sidhe will know her!" she cried.
"Midir will know her, if only by her song!"

So Femnach raised a wind that came beneath the butterfly's wings.
It lifted Etain higher and higher until at last she reached the halls of
heaven. There she landed on the palm of Aengus Og, keeper of the
birds. Because Aengus knew all the winged creatures of the world, he
recognized Etain immediately.

"Alas," he cried. "Who has taken you away from Midir and the
fairy folk?"

"Femnach the witch woman," Etain replied. "Can you send me
back to my people?"

"I do not have the power to break this spell," Aengus said sadly,
"but I can keep you safe with me in the halls of heaven."

So Aengus built Etain a crystal garden with trees of prisms and pearls
and flowers like stained glass windows in the sunlight. He brought her
the finest honey and grasses and beseeched all the birds of heaven to
keep the harsh winds away from her with the strength of their wings.
There, in the garden of Aengus Og, Etain stayed for many years,
humming such sad songs that it made Aengus weep to hear them.

Below, in the land of the sidhe, Midir no longer threw back his head and
laughed aloud. By the dark of night the fairy folk could hear him weeping
for his lost Etain. By day he would don his white cloak, saddle his white
horse, and ride to all the corners of Eire searching for his lost beloved.

Only Femnach was happy. She believed that Etain was dead.

One day Aengus Og had to travel to the world of the sidhe.

"Take me with you," begged Etain. "Let me look just once more upon
the people of the sidhe and I will be able to sing joyful songs again."

Aengus Og could not resist such a promise, so he took Etain with
him, resting lightly on his palm. When he reached Eire, he placed her
gently on the petals of a red rose while he went about his business. So

overjoyed was Etain to be among the roses of Eire that she began to hum a happy song.

Femnach was passing by and heard her.

"I believed that you were dead!" she cried. "Midir must not find you here."

Once again Femnach raised a wind, this one mightier than the first. It spun Etain past the world of the sidhe, past the halls of heaven, far, far east, into the world of humans.

Upon hearing the wind, Aengus Og returned and found Etain gone.

"What have you done?" he cried to Femnach.

When Femnach did not answer, Aengus knew that she had cast another spell on Etain. He grew very angry. He called to him all the birds of the world and they came swooping about the witch woman—gulls and eagles, hawks and crows—their wings flapping a terrible wind.

"Become what you wished for Etain!" cried Aengus Og.

Up and around spun the witch woman, trapped in the body of a black and ugly crow. Even now you can hear her cawing her anger at Aengus Og.

But Etain was gone.

For many days, the wind that Femnach had cast continued, buffeting Etain wildly above the world. Finally, after three long days, she fluttered to rest on the high broad beam of a castle ceiling.

Below her, the humans were having a feast. Their table was set with gold and crystal, piled high with sweets and honeyed bread. Etain was hungry and leaned forward to glimpse the feast. Just as she did, the wind caught at her again.

Down and down she spiraled, into the cup of the human queen. Just then, the queen lifted the wine to her lips and drank. Nine months later, the queen gave birth to a beautiful baby daughter with hair the copper of autumn leaves and skin as white as the wings of swans. She named the child Etain.

Etain grew up gentle and kind, with a voice as sweet as the harps of heaven, but she no longer remembered Midir or that she was the queen of the fairy folk. Only her heart remembered, for each evening she would stand at the high tower window of the castle, looking off to the west. Then, she would sing such sad and longing songs that the humans would weep to hear them.

Etain's beauty brought many offers of marriage. At last, her parents decided to give her hand to young King Echu of Tara. Etain pleaded with them to change their minds.

"I do not belong with this man," she cried. "I will only bring him sorrow."

"Tell us then the man that you would choose," her mother asked her.

Etain did not know and could not remember. In due time, Etain was married to Echu. Now Echu admired Etain's great beauty and her lovely voice. He was as kind to her as a human king can be. But Echu's great love was his kingdom—his castles and horses and warriors and most importantly, his gold. He spent his hours fighting, riding, and counting his coffers of gold.

Each evening Etain stood alone and lonely at the high tower window, staring off to the west and singing such sad and longing songs that it made the people weep to hear them.

One evening when Etain was singing at her tower window, she saw a handsome young man in a white cloak, riding a white horse toward the castle. Immediately, Etain ceased her singing, her heart beating wildly within her, though she did not know why. She ran to the great hall to meet the stranger.

Midir, for he was indeed the rider, saw Etain coming down the great stair. For the first time in all his years of searching, he threw back his head and laughed aloud, a sound of so much joy that all the assembled people laughed with him.

"What can we give you, stranger?" Echu asked. "For you have made us glad of heart."

"One thing only," Midir replied. "I ask that you play me a game of fidchell. If you win, I will give you my bag of gold." He hefted a bag of gold onto the table and the bright coins spilled into the light. "But if I win the game, I ask but one kiss from your queen."

"One kiss is not so great a thing," said Echu, eyeing the gold. But he stared uneasily at Etain, who could not take her eyes from the stranger.

So they set up the patchwork board with its pieces of silver and gold and they played long into the flickering firelight hours. At last, Midir won the game. When he stepped toward Etain to claim his prize, Echu changed his mind.

"Nay!" he cried. "She belongs to me. You shall not kiss her."

But Midir's lips had touched Etain's. In that moment she remembered all.

"Midir, my husband, my love," she cried. Then she burst into a song so joyful that it rivaled the harps of heaven.

When Echu heard the song, he knew that Etain would leave with Midir.

"Stop them!" he cried to his warriors. The warriors drew their swords and rushed toward the couple, but Midir threw his white cloak around Etain. In a sudden rush of wind, Midir and Etain disappeared. When Echu and his company ran outside the castle to search for them, Midir and Etain were nowhere to be found.

High above the castle tower, two white swans circled against the starlit sky then flew toward the west, far, far toward the magical country of the sidhe.

The Three Phases of Etain

The lovely story above is our retelling of the Etain myth from our book *The Story We Carry in Our Bones: Irish History for Americans*. It definitely has a mythic, romantic "star-crossed lovers" tone that has made it a popular story with Americans. But the truth of the Etain myth is far more complicated and threads itself across multiple time periods and themes that are much darker than the story above might lead us to believe. The full story of *The Wooing of Etain* occurs in three stages:

Part One

- Etain, of course, is the fairest woman of all the land. We all expect this from our myths. But in part one, Midir, kind of the Tuatha de Danaan (the fair folk or little people) claims her as payment for a debt, despite the fact that he is already married. Meanwhile, the god Aengus wins her by clearing rivers and plains in Ireland.
- Femnach, in this version of the story, is Midir's original wife and she is none too pleased. She turns Etain into a pool of water. When the pool dries up, Etain remains as a purple fly.
- Nonetheless, Midir wants her with him, so Femnach blows Etain out to sea for seven years, except that the wind deposits her on the tunic of Aengus, who keeps her in a crystal cage and feeds her flowers.
- When Femnach discovers this, she blows Etain away again,

whereby she falls from a beam into the cup of Étar, the human wife of the King of Ulster.

Part Two

- A thousand years pass. Eochaid Airem becomes king of Ireland and asks for the fairest woman in all the land. Of course, they bring him Etain, who has no idea that she is one of the sidhe.
- Meanwhile, Eochaid's brother Aillil is lovesick for Etain and she agrees to a tryst to cure him. Three times, she tries to meet him outside the castle and three times he sleeps through the tryst.
- However, Midir, king of the sidhe, shows up at the tryst, tells her who she is and asks her to return to him, but she says that she will not go without her husband's permission.

Does this imply that he gave her permission for the trysting with his poor, lovesick brother?

Part Three

Here, the story begins to resemble our story above—that is, until it doesn't.

- A warrior in a purple tunic comes to Eochaid Arem carrying a spear and a shield, and he asks to play fidchell (an ancient Irish form of chess) with Eochaid. He allows Eochaid to win three times, each time giving him gold

Towers feature prominently in the myth cycle of Ireland as you have already seen in several of our stories. Whether this is a holdover from Norman occupation, and thus a later interpolation into the stories, or whether it results from the wild sea stacks off the Irish coast is anyone's guess.

and silver. The warrior, is, of course, Midir. When they play the fourth game, Midir wins. As his prize, he asks for a kiss from Etain.

- Eochaid is suspicious at this point and tells Midir he must wait a month. However, at the end of the month, he gathers all his warriors and locks the tower.
- Midir appears in the hall, despite the locks and warriors, kisses Etain and turns the two of them into wild swans and disappears through the upper tower window.
- However, the story doesn't end here. Desperate to get Etain back, Eochaid and his warriors dig up Bri Leith, the fairy mound in which Midir lives. To save the underground city of the Others, Midir agrees to return Etain, but instead sends fifty clones. He says that Eochaid must choose the true Etain to get her back, but Eochaid chooses Etain's daughter, who looks exactly like Etain.
- The Oedipal twist in this part of the tale, is that Eochaid has accidentally chosen his own daughter, because Etain was pregnant when she departed with Midir and time passes much differently among the sidhe.
- Eochaid impregnates his own daughter and then discovers that she is his daughter. Horrified, Eochaid sets his daughter aside and puts the baby out in the hills to die. The baby is discovered and raised by a herdsman and his wife and in a later myth becomes the mother of Irish High King Conaire Mór.

Kind of takes all of the romance out of the story, doesn't it?

The Curse of Macha Fleet Foot

For Crunniuc it was the loneliness. The terrible loneliness.

He loved his children, surely. He worried for them when he was herding the cattle or driving them to the river. Worrying that they would burn themselves on the lodge fire. Worrying that there was no order in his hut. Worrying that there was never prepared food, that they were like animals foraging, day and night.

He had not expected his young wife to die and now it had been more than a year.

He missed her snug form, braced against him in the bed. He missed a tidy house and prepared food. But more than all of these, he missed her conversation, for Crunniuc was a man who loved to talk.

He sighed and leaned against his staff. The light was going down; it was time to herd the cattle home, to fend as best he could for his motherless children.

As he approached his little hut, he saw smoke curling from the chimney. Crunniuc broke into a run. He flung the door open.

The hut was tidy. All the children's clothes were hung neatly on the pegs. A savory stew simmered in the cauldron over the fire.

And there beside that cauldron sat a woman, stirring and singing, the children at her feet, playing with their little toys.

Crunniuc stood stock still.

The woman was beautiful. Her long hair was blacker than smoke, blacker than a moonless night. Even when she looked up at him, her eyes were black, as though they had no pupils.

"I have heard of the death of your dear wife," she said in a smoky voice. "I have come to care for you and for your children. I will be your new wife. You may call me Macha. And now, do tell me of your day."

Crunniuc had not thought it possible to be deliriously happy, to be—and here he winced to think it—happier than he had been with the mother of his own children.

But the beautiful Macha spoke little and listened to him always, hanging on his every word as though it were mead from a silver cup. His little hut was spotless, his children clean and well-dressed, well-fed, happy, and safe.

In fact, the only time she spent apart from him was when she ran along the river. Oh how he loved to watch her run, his Macha Fleet Foot. It seemed to him that she moved like the wind, that she swept above the ground, so effortless was her gait, so wild her speed that horses could not outpace her.

And now the beautiful Macha was pregnant. Twins, she told him, though how she knew that he did not know and dared not ask.

And then the invitation—well, it was a summons—came from the High King of Ulster Conor Mac Nessa. All of Ulster knew of Conor and his formidable fighting machine, his Craobh Rua, the Red Branch of Ulster. One did not decline his invitation, though Crunniuc sorely wished to. He wanted nothing more than to stay warm and well-fed, tucked into bed beside his beautiful Macha.

Now, for the first time, she spoke at length.

"They are braggarts all, the Craobh Rua. And the worst of them is Conor. He is that most terrible of kings, a narcissist, who thinks that he is first in all things. Hear me Crunniuc. They will tell stories and brag. They will slaver over their haunches of deer and down their mead, and when they are in their cups, their stories will take on proportions that no human story should have. They are not gods, these warrior boys. No, they are not gods. But they believe themselves to be so."

Crunniuc was so surprised by her oratory, that for once he said nothing at all.

"You are actually a good man Crunniuc. Simple and hard-working. I love your children as I will love my own,"—and here she patted her growing belly—"but oh you do love to talk. Heed me now. When you are among the warriors of Conor, when you sit at Conor's table, say nothing of me. Say not one word. For if you do, I fear that tragedy will follow."

The feast went on for three full days!

There were storytellers and jugglers, genealogists who could tell the history of every clan. There were singers and harpists and even twelve finely dressed lawyers hearing case after case while they drank beer or mead at a long trestle table in the king's hall.

Crunniuc thought that he had never seen so much food. There was wild boar roasted on a spit, tender venison cooked in the boiling pit called fulacht fiadh. Honey mead, little cakes with finely ground nuts drizzled in honey, followed leeks and berries and salmon fresh from the river.

He was tempted to brag on the cooking skills of his beautiful wife, but though it took everything he had, he remembered her warning and held his tongue.

The races began on the third day.

On the track that circled the high hill, there were children's foot races and women's. The warriors of the Craobh Rua thundered through the dust, passing a baton. Horses raced against each other and then chariots, often with the drivers standing on the bar between the horses while the charioteer steered from behind. These were dizzying feats of skill, but still Crunniuc held his tongue, knowing in his heart of hearts that his beautiful wife would have won every race, even against the lathered horses.

And then, on the last race of the last day, King Conor Mac Nessa brought forth his own pair of horses and his own chariot.

"Who will wager against my grays?" he called to the assembled crowd.

For a time there was a silence and then the two fastest charioteers took the wager. "We will, great king," they called. "We will try your legendary pair."

Conor Mac Nessa wheeled his own chariot onto the wide track and waited while the two horsemen came up to either side.

The king cut a fine figure, Crunniuc observed, as he filled his cup of mead for the fourth time. Conor Mac Nessa was dressed in the seven colors of kingship. He wore plaid braichs in a woven blue and green, with leather sandals laced up to nearly his knees. His cloak was of a different weave entirely, a deep burgundy and a smoky gray, caught with a huge penannular brooch at this shoulder. Beneath his cloak, his embroidered tunic gleamed with a scene of intertwined horses, their legs braided and interwoven in patterns too complex to unweave, silver and gold tied together endlessly. Of course, he wore the golden circlet of his kingship over his dark hair.

The horses, for their part, pranced and jingled, so anxious were they to run the great race.

At the signal, the three chariots leapt forward, then thundered down the course. It was to no one's surprise that the chariot of King Conor came to the finish line two lengths before the chariots of his fellow competitors.

"Ho ho!" he cried out to the assembled crowd. "There is none in all of Eire who could beat my prancing grays! Give them their due!"

But before the crowd could raise the general shout, Crunniuc heard the words come out of his mouth.

"My wife could beat your grays," he said.

There was a long, long pause while Conor Mac Nessa turned his kingly head in Crunniuc's direction.

"Your wife?" he said, his tone all disbelief. "Your wife is a charioteer?"

"No," said Crunniuc, "I have misspoken." And now his heart was beating so hard that he had to press his palm against it to stop the thundering staccato.

"How misspoken, cattleman?"

Crunniuc did not reply.

"How misspoken cattleman?" Conor thundered. "Speak now or I will have your tongue."

Crunniuc hung his head, but he answered truly. "Great King, my wife, barefoot and with no horses, could beat your pair—and yes, even your chariot with you as driver. So fleet is she of foot."

Crunniuc felt relief sweep over him when the king laughed. Perhaps, after all, he would escape the fate of his own loose tongue.

But then the king spoke again.

"Well, bring her to us then that we may see the fleet foot woman who can beat the horses of a king!"

When she came before the king, Macha would not look at Crunniuc at all. It was as though he did not exist, had never existed.

But the men of Ulster were stunned that a mere cattleman could be married to such a beauty. Her hair was a waterfall of obsidian black, her skin like moonlight, her eyes the dark of drowning.

"Your husband tells us that you can defeat me and my chariot and horses. That you can do this horseless and barefoot." the king called out. There was a humor in his face, but it was cruel.

Now Macha removed her cloak, letting it drop into the dust. The women gathered about on the hilltop gasped, for she was clearly pregnant, her belly a ripe mound of some seven moons.

"Men of Ulster!" she called aloud. "You see before you a woman heavy with child, a woman who was wed to an unworthy man. Each of you has come here through the loins of a woman. Spare me any trial that would cost the lives of these children."

And though many of the Red Branch warriors hung their heads in shame, King Conor Mac Nessa had already yoked his grays and leapt into his chariot in all of his finery.

"No one challenges me without making good on that challenge," he called.

The woman moved quietly to a spot parallel to his horses.

"Good King," cried several of the women. "Spare her this race until the child is born. You will only need wait two moons."

"Nay!" he cried "We have been challenged. We will rise to that challenge."

And the signal was given.

There was no contest. Everyone on the hill saw that immediately. The woman floated before the horses, her hair streaming behind her, her legs churning like the wind on the sea cliffs. She reached the finish line even before the horses had made the turn. But there she fell. Fell into a heap on the ground, screaming in pain. Some of the women rushed to her aid, parted her legs, but those poor children were stillborn, covered in blood.

Now the woman gathered the tiny infants into her arms, winding them into her cloak.

"Know who I am great King," she called. "For I am Macha, goddess of war and these are mine—my sisters and my children—all of us immortal."

She leapt to the top of a rock in a single movement and shook out her black cloak. On her shoulder appeared a black raven, emerging from the windings of the cloak and around them both swirled a dark and foreboding wind.

"For this act against the most sacred task of womanhood I curse you!"

She pointed first at the quaking king and then at all the warriors of the Red Branch.

"For nine generations, I curse you! When your country needs you most, when battle calls and your own wives and children are in danger, you will suffer nine days of labor pains from which you will not, cannot rise."

"Here now, share your fate and show your women your worthlessness."

With that, she swept her hand over the assembled company.

King Conor Mac Nessa and all of the men of the Red Branch fell to the ground, writhing in screaming pain, for the children they would never bear and for the great evil they had done to Macha Fleet Foot.

The legends will tell you that this is why Cú Chulainn was born to the County of Ulster, but more of him to come. The legends will tell you that this is why to this day that great hill is known as Emain Macha, the twins of Macha. But more of that to come.

For Macha had vanished from their midst.

And for Crunniuc it was the loneliness. The terrible, endless loneliness.

The Children of Lir

Oh, there is a sorrow in the telling.

For long ago, fado fado, when the magical people of Ireland still lived on the surface of the land, there lived a wise and good king named Lir. Beloved to Lir was his gentle wife, and his children four: Aodh, Conn, Fiachra, and the beautiful Fionnula, his only daughter who cared for her brothers with open arms.

And then Lir's beloved wife, the mother of his children, died.

Lir's father-in-law, Bodb the Red, watched the little family mourn and finally could not bear their sorrow.

So he brought before Lir his seven remaining daughters.

"It is not good," he said, "that you should be alone. Nor should my grandchildren be without a mother's care. Choose from my daughters any one, for all of them have agreed to be your bride."

And Lir chose Aoife, the most beautiful of the daughters of Bodb.

Great beauty does not always guarantee great kindness, for the human face is not always mated to the human heart. And Aoife was jealous. She could not bear Lir's great love for his children, could not bear that he loved his children more than her.

In the summer, she began to take the children swimming each day in the cool and beautiful waters of Lake Derravaragh.

One day, when the children were far out on the water, Aoife called a wind.

Soft as eiderdown the wind she called, streaming from the sprung white clouds above the water.

But as that wind passed over the children, all of them could feel a tugging in their shoulder blades. Their arms tucked back behind them; white feathers sprouted from their skin. By the time that wind had passed, the children of Lir had vanished from the water. All that remained were four beautiful white swans. And then she called the curse upon them:

Nine hundred years I curse you
To wander o'er the waters of the world.
The first three hundred years Derravaragh,
The second three the wild Sea of Moyle,
The last three hundred years on Inishglora.

But Aoife had forgotten the most important thing, for she did not take from the children the gifts of human speech and song.

Aoife returned to the castle alone. She pretended her worry, saying, "Our beloved children were swimming and now I cannot find them anywhere."

Lir was terrified. He swung himself astride his horse and lifted Aoife behind him. He rode down to the edge of the water, but there were no children, only four white swans drifting through the watery reeds at the far side of the lake.

Now he gathered all his soldiers. His father-in-law Bodb the Red joined the search, standing in his saddle, calling the names of his grandchildren, his voice growing more hoarse with every pass around the lake.

Night fell. Lir and Bodh built a bothy by the water. They lit a little driftwood fire. Together they sat, watching the moonlight stream across the rippling lake. Between them, Aoife was satisfied. Though she pretended heavy sorrow, she had achieved her goal.

But then, across the water, came the sound of singing and the voice was Fionnula's.

Lir leapt to his feet.

"Daughter," he called. "Come to me. Oh come to me bearing your brothers."

And into the flickering light of the fire swam four beautiful swans.

"Father, we are here," said Fionnula, "but we are sorely changed."

"Who has done this?" thundered Bodb the Red. "Give me the name that I may slay him now."

Now Aoife was terrified. She leapt to her feet. She would have run for the horses, but Fionnula stayed her with her words.

"You daughter has done this grandfather. Your daughter Aoife the beautiful."

Bodb leapt to his feet. "Undo this curse, you evil child," he cried.

But Aoife only shook her head. "I cannot break the curse, for it is binding. Binding for nine hundred years."

"I bind you then," cried Bodb. "Nine hundred years alone. Nine hundred years, the wind that moves across the western sea." He smashed his stick upon the ground and cell by cell his daughter broke apart and vanished, carried out to the western sea, where all could hear her wailing out her sorrow.

But nothing more could be done.

Lir and Bodb built a dwelling there beside the water. All day one of them, or both, walked the shores of the beautiful lake, speaking to the feathered swans who once had been their children. As for Fionnula, when the nights were cold or there was no moon, she sheltered all her brothers well beneath her wings. And so, three hundred years passed by.

With that time, went the time of the magical people of Ireland, forced beneath the ground by the coming of the humans to the emerald isle of Eire.

And so, the four children were forced to go alone to the Sea of Moyle.

Oh, the sea of Moyle is a stormy sea and cold. Here the waters heave, heave between Eire and Alba. No place here is gentle enough for swans. Fionnula's work was hard in that wild and windy sea, for often she would tuck her brothers into the lea of a little bay, hold them close beneath her wings, and let the winds howl over them. And on that wild sea, the children mourned the loss of their father and grandfather, of gentle Lake Derravaragh, of the time of the magical people of Ireland.

At last, when three hundred years had passed, the children were swept at last to Inishglora off the western coast of wide Mayo.

Gentle were the winds on the green island, warm the island waters. Gentle too and joyful was the one who had built his monastery there. For though the time of the little people had vanished, the time of the good Christ had come and Brendan was his Navigator.

Day by day, Fionnula watched the monk as he walked by the water and ticked his beads. He was generous to the swan children, feeding them the moisty grass and sometimes bringing worms from the turning earth.

At last, Fionnula knew that Brendan was a man who would not fear a wonder. So, on a warm spring afternoon, she glided close and when the monk came to sit beside the water, she gathered her courage and spoke.

"I see," she said, "that this world fills your heart with wonder."

At first he leapt to his feet and looked about, for the only inhabitants of the island were Brendan and his holy brothers. But at last, he sat back down.

"You have spoken to me," he said, regarding the beautiful swan.

"Once I was a child," Fionnula said. "Once my brothers and I played as you played. But in the long ago time, the magical time that passed, we were cursed by a darkling woman, trapped in the forms you see before you."

"How long?" the monk asked. "How long child?"

"Nine hundred years," Fionnula replied.

Now Brendan's heart was greatly moved. He leapt to his feet and ran to his little oratory, returning with a vessel of holy water.

"Shall I cast this water over you?" he asked. "For it is holy and will remove this curse that binds you now."

Fionnula nodded her assent, but she whispered to Brendan. "We may not be free for long. Too many centuries have passed, even for the people of the Tuatha de Danaan."

So Brendan shook the water over them and as he watched, their arms appeared beneath their feathers. The sturdy legs of childhood bore them back to land. One by one they arose out of their swan forms, children, beautiful and whole.

But then, before another breath, they began to crumple and fold. Their skin grew withered and old, and they fell to the earth that they had longed for all those years.

"Brendan," Fionnula whispered. "Bury my brothers beneath my arms, for just so I have kept them safe these centuries of exile."

And good Brendan did just as she had asked.

Still, the people of Inishglora say that when the moon is full, when the wind is right upon the water, they hear Fionnula singing, singing to her brothers of the world that once they knew.

Syncretization and the Pagan/Christian Shift

In *The Children of Lir* we have what is called a syncretization tale, a tale that puts together two storylines and two timelines that can't really go together, but they do. Why?

Because this is a tale of pagan/Christian shift.

We would have none of these stories were it not for the monks who copied them down, laboring away in their beehive huts and oratories, preserving the stories on vellum and especially in the vernacular—Irish.

But how could these new Christians justify a tale of magic and curses, of forces that they purported to no longer believe? The answer is in the blend, in giving a pagan tale a Christian twist or in acknowledging the presence of a pagan element in a Christian tale. Often, then, the new religion and the old religion become intertwined in these tales, a feature that we take for granted in much early literature like *Beowulf* or like these syncretized Irish myths.

So, there are many versions of Lir, with and without the Christian bookends, substituting St. Patrick for St. Brendan and so on. The miraculous thing is that we still have the stories and can pass them along.

The beehive cell of an early monk. Churches or oratories were built in the same style.

Chapter 3

Myths of the Shift to Human Time

Deichtine and the Golden Birds

The birds were never golden.

That is the way of stories, is it not? Someone tells the aftertale, someone with a longing heart or someone with a blighted mind, someone who cannot separate the truth from the tale. And so the story changes, shapes around the tongue of every teller.

I was a charioteer. My brother's charioteer. And my brother was the king of Ulster. You know surely what that meant for me. All the men who could not fathom a woman who drove the horses into lather, a woman who could stand across the bars that yoked the horses. A fearless woman. A woman who dressed in braichs and tied her hair in a single braid like a man.

My brother is Conor Mac Nessa, a king who is sometimes beloved and sometimes feared. A king whose cloak trails the gossip of all of Ulster behind him. Surely, you have heard it all. That I was only his charioteer because we were more than brother and sister.

Faugh.

As if a woman could not handle a pair of prancing horses.

Still, on the strength of that rumor, Conor betrothed me to Súaldem, a good man, a stolid man of simple thoughts who wanted nothing more than a quiet woman by his fire. I was good to Súaldem and kind. I let him think the choice of betrothal was mine. He did not deserve the trouble my brother always dragged in his kingly wake.

And so, time passed. Súaldem wished for a child and I gave him every opportunity, but no child came. I too began to long for a babe. And then came the sunset of the birds.

Some storytellers say that they were golden birds, linked together in the sky by braids of golden rope. Others paint a tale of a vast flock of wild swans, backlit by an autumn moon, their wings vanishing in the clouds.

They were crows.

They led me all the way to Brúgh na Bóinne.

I drove the chariot myself. I zigged and zagged across that field, so freshly planted, all the crows feasting on the seed. My brother charioteers drove with me, all of us saving the seed, driving the crows from the crop. But those dark birds moved before us like a plague, rising and falling, so dense that they obscured the evening sky.

I know now that they were messengers. Their purpose was Cú Chulainn, the war boy I would bear. But I did not know that then. I thought only to save the fields. And too, there was the joy of driving my team across the fields and back, of feeling the chariot swerve and heave and hew again to the earth.

I was surprised when I came to Brúgh na Bóinne for it was twenty leagues away.

But Lugh was waiting there and he opened his palm and helped me from my chariot. I was struck dumb, for in Lugh the stories beggar truth. More beautiful than any human was Lugh Lamhfada. Nigh to seven feet tall, the sinews of his arms like stone, his great hands gentle as a zephyr. When Lugh stood tall, his red-gold hair cascaded around his red beard, his long mustache drooped below the line of his cheeks. He was radiant to behold. And above all his eyes—blue like the ice of the mountain sky. Clear. So full of knowledge.

I did not ask him why he had called me, for I knew by then that the birds were an invitation. I am the daughter of a druid mother and no one's fool.

I have learned since that the birds were Morrigu herself, mirroring her image again and again, drawing me forward to the war boy that she herself would love more than any other human. Had I known then that she was leading me on, I might not have followed. But then I thought the birds had come from Lugh.

He held my hand in his, spoke softly. "We must make a hero, Deichtine, a boy from the legacy of the Tuatha de Danaan, a boy from the line of human kings. Because the day is coming when he must be the saving of Ulster. The day is coming when the wild queen of Connacht will plunge this country into war. On that day, the men of Ulster will be laid low, felled by the pains of labor, subject to the ancient curse. And this boy, this boy that we will make, must be their saving."

Some storytellers will tell you that I crushed that boy in my very womb. Some will say I drank the boy like a bug in my cups.

How foolish do they think you are?

I stretched my length along the length of Lugh and together we made the boy, his son and mine.

When I returned to Súaldem, I took to my wheel and my looms. He grew frightened then, wondering why I was not at my chariot. But I told him that we were expecting a child. I feared for the birth of the child, because I did not want to shame Súaldem, this good and stolid man. I thought that the boy would look like Lugh, that on the day of his birth everyone in Ulster would know. Again, I was wrong. For the child looked like Súaldem, short and barrel-bodied, his unruly hair swirling around a face that clearly bore Súaldem's bulbous nose. My child was as unprepossessing as Lugh, his father, was beautiful.

And so, I too began to think that it had all been a dream, that I had imagined the wild fields of crows, the moonlit ride, that I had imagined Lugh. Something in me came to believe that the child was truly the child of Súaldem.

Do you see what a gift that was to my boy? For he would have an ordinary childhood, among a tribe who loved him.

We called him Setanta, a name which means "one who knows the ways." For seven years he lived a perfectly normal life, though some of the boys made fun of him for his short stature, for his unruly hair.

And then we learned with certainty that our lad was not ordinary. For then, he earned his new name, his true identity.

At eight years old, he became Cú Chulainn.

The Hound of Ulster.

The Morrigu, who often shapeshifts as a crow or raven, is heavily involved in the life of Cú Chulainn, as we will see in our "Legends" section.

The Coming of the Milesians

Long ago or longer, in a kingdom known as Eire by the sea, there lived a magical people called the Tuatha de Danaan. They never grew sick, and they never grew old, and they had lived on the land from time out of mind.

But from the sea in their great ships came the nine sons of Mil. Stalwart they were, and warlike, these Celts from the coast of Galicia.

Some of the Tuatha de Danaan, knowing that the Milesians would come, and soon, proposed that they disappear beneath the earth and under the mounds. But some, and Morrigu among them, proposed to destroy the humans before they could get a foothold on the land.

And land they did, at the Bay of Kenmare, with their horses and their cows, their wailing children and their brawling brothers.

They saw the Tuatha at once, standing on the headland, their white cloaks shifting in the winds, saw too the dark trio among them.

"We must destroy them," the brothers whispered to each other. "For surely, these are people of power. Small as they are, can we not see their power? We must attack before they come down the headlands toward us."

And so they leapt to the backs of their horses, and raced up the headland, spears drawn. But when they reached the crest of the hill, they were met by a trio of women of extraordinary beauty, who were in no way afraid.

"Will you make war against us?" the sisters asked them. "We who have done you no harm? We who could help you here on the green island?"

One of the brothers—the poet Amergin—counseled wisdom. "Brothers," he said, "the way of war is not always the wisest path.

What if these could indeed become our friends and allies?"

And the brothers, after conferring, decided on a compromise. They would give the shining people three days to prepare. And then they would come against them.

"Please," the sisters begged them. "We do not remember how to make war, for we have lived in peace here for nigh on a thousand years. Retreat to your ships and allow us to confer."

The Milesians did so, rowing their landing boats out to the great ships that lay at anchor, gathering their families on the great decks of the biremes, but leaving their cattle and their horses behind. Then they drew up sail and retreated to the ninth wave of the sea, just as the sisters had requested.

And when they were far out on the water, the little people of the Tuatha de Danaan raised up a fog. The fog slipped down from the headland and obscured the shore. It crept over the water and obscured the sea. At last, it obscured the ships, each from the other. Frightened, the Milesians raised their sails, tried to sail back into the open sea, some trying to return to Galicia. But it was too late. The ships were dashed on the rocks, were dashed against each other. And when the fog lifted at last, five of the nine sons of Mil were drowned.

Oh, the remaining brothers were angry. They rowed their currachs into the bay, they flung themselves onto the backs of their horses. By the hundreds, the warriors of Galicia thundered up the headlands. The drove the fleeing Tuatha de Danaan before them, followed them all the way to a great circle of stones. There, the doorways separated the human world from the world of the Other, human time from time out of mind.

In a great battle there, in the stone circle, the humans defeated the little people of Ireland, binding them hand and foot, circling the sisters who were clearly their leaders.

"Kill them!" some called.

"Banish them from the green island!" others cried.

But Amergin, the poet, stepped forward.

And ah, the power of the poets to the Celts of Milesia. For Amergin knew that his words could stop the war.

And Amergin had looked into the eyes of the little people. He knew that they possessed *an draíocht,* the magic. And he knew that if they departed the green isle, the magic would go with them.

So he proposed a compromise.

"Brothers," he cried. "Exile these who have cost us our brothers.

Yes. But exile them here, that their magic can dwell beside us. Give them the hollows beneath the hills and the cities that are hidden beneath waves of the sea."

When the brothers agreed, the little people stepped into the stone doorways in the great sarsen circle and vanished.

And to this day, yes this very day, they have lived beside and beneath the people of Eire.

And because they have remained, the magic remains on the island.

Is fírinne sinn; this is the truth of my telling.

Would you like to hear a telling of this story?
Visit https://www.youtube.com/watch?v=TwrUsU-Ek6U.

Human (Historical) Time

The Milesians of Galicia evidently did come to Ireland around 500 BC, landing in the Bay of Kenmare, as recent DNA may indicate. It looks as though they spread throughout Ireland and even Scotland, building *brochs*, or towers, that match those on the Iberian Peninsula of Spain.

They were not the first human invaders to come to the emerald island, nor would they be the last. Geneticists now speculate that the Irish genetic makeup includes Norse DNA as well as Norman, French, and even Sardinian.

However, the myth of the Milesian battle against the little people has been passed down for thousands of years.

The Song of Amergin

Supposedly Amergin, the poet of the Milesians, spontaneously chanted the poem below when he landed in Ireland. You will see it in many, many translations, but it first appeared in the *Lebhor Gabhala* (See Mythology: Whoo Wants to Know More?). We don't really know when or where it originated, but whoever wrote it has a clear sense of Celtic panentheism—that God is everywhere and contains all things, omnipresent, beautifully abundant, worthy of awe.

Most Common English Translation
Song of Amergin

I am the wind on the sea,
I am the wave on the water,
I am the sigh of the billows,
I am a stag of seven tines
I am the eagle on the rocks,
I am a beam of the sun,
I am the loveliest of plants,
I am a wild boar in bravery,
I am a salmon in a pool,
I am a lake on a plain,
I am the word of poetry,
I am the point of the battle-lance,
I am the God who puts fire in the mind.
Who throws light onto the mountain?
Who knows the secrets of the dolmen?
Who announces the ages of the moon?
Who teaches the resting place of the sun?
If not I?

Medieval Irish
Song of Amergin

Am gaeth i m-muir,
Am tond trethan,
Am fuaim mara,
Am dam secht ndirend,
Am séig i n-aill,
Am dér gréne,
Am cain lubai,
Am torc ar gail,
Am he i l-lind,
Am loch i m-maig,
Am brí a ndai,
Am bri danae,
Am bri i fodb fras feochtu,
Am dé delbas do chind codnu,
Cia on co tagair aesa éscai?
Cia du i l-laig fuiniud gréne?

Myths

Whooo wants to know more?

What Is Mythology?

Brilliant Celtic scholar Marie Sjoestedt said that "Romans think of their myths historically; the Irish think of their history mythologically." What this means for the Irish is that every place in Ireland is the site of a myth, the place of a story. Thus, landscape and story are sacred and fraught with meaning, even now. Thus, myth and legend are the basis of everything.

Joseph Campbell was fond of saying that myth is what we call other people's religion.

But myth is not precisely religion. Nor is myth belief, exactly. Belief exists underneath myth. Belief is an acknowledgement that something exists which is not us. Humans intuit, across almost all cultures, that something larger or more encompassing, older and more knowledgeable is moving in/through/behind the universe. Myth tries to codify what that is.

Once, at a writer's picnic, I was seated at a table with a Zen Buddhist monk. Talk turned, as it often does with writers, to God. The monk gave the best analogy I have ever heard: "To not believe in the existence of God, would be to believe that a tornado could sweep through your town, depart, and leave in its wake a perfectly functioning amusement park that did not exist before the tornado." In other words, the evidence for the existence of a highly complex and organized universe is just too overwhelming to ignore.

Myth attempts to answer the questions that such awareness inevitably raises. What is the nature of that intelligence? Can we trust it? Is it kind or punitive? Who are we? Why were we put here? What is our purpose? What is our relationship to It? Does it all matter? If so, in what ways does it matter?

Cultures tend to answer those questions in a wide variety of ways, often with answers that reflect their own underlying cultural norms. In other words, they anthropomorphize their gods, making the gods like them.

Greek gods, for example, interact with each other and with humans in ways that are brutal, selfish, punitive, and warlike. Gods are condemned to rolling endless rocks, living below the earth for half the year, even dwelling in hell. Gods brutalize their human charges. Why? Are the Greeks excusing their own behavior by making the behavior of their gods equally venal and still more terrifying? Are they explaining dualism? Light and darkness? Good and evil? Suffering? Certainly, the Greeks thought and wrote about all these issues.

The Romans adopted that same Greek Olympiad of gods, renaming them for their own purposes. In fact, the Romans were fond of adopting and adapting gods from almost every culture they encountered, evidently unwilling or unable to create a pantheon of their own, beyond their Romulus and Remus origin myth. The Greek Artemis, goddess of the hunt, for example, becomes the Roman Diana. Ares, the Greek god of war, becomes the Roman Mars. When the Romans encountered the Celts, who professed belief in a water goddess called Sulis, the Romans immediately adopted Sulis, conflated her with their water goddess Minerva and began calling the holy bath of Sulis in Bath, England, by the name Minerva/Sulis. When it comes to the gods, we can think of the Romans as being on a scale from adaptive to *laissez-faire.*

Most cultures are less adaptive than the Romans, tending to define and restrict their gods by their own cultural norms and behaviors. So, the Norse (and pan-Germanic) god, Thor, is a hammer-wielder, a warrior, a defender of humans, a maker of thunder and lightning. He is the perfect god for the warrior cultures who espouse him. His fellow god Loki is more complex; often referred to as a "trickster," he answers questions of consistency and purpose. He "explains" the quixotic and untrustworthy nature of experience. He is a shapeshifter whose escapades range from noble to comic, from deep suffering to tragedy. Additionally, Ragnarök (what we might call Apocalypse or Armageddon) broods over the whole trajectory of Norse myth, as does Valhalla, which requires a warrior's death as its entrance ticket.

Trickster figures also exist in many Native American cultures; coyote for example, can run the gamut from a figure of humor, to a dangerous and dark skin-walking shapeshifter, as can Iktomi among the Lakota, or Gluscaube among the Abenaki, a god of making who can deal with humans in ways that are capricious, funny, or punitive.

All of these examples go back to the original set of needs and questions: Who are we? What is our purpose? Why is life so difficult and unpredictable? Who will protect us from all of this? Can we actually rely on or trust any of these gods?

A myth, then, is a pathway. The wanderer on that pathway is seeking answers and the myth is one path toward those answers. The interesting thing is that most, if not all, cultures throughout human history have invented and reinvented, fleshed out, and codified a set of myths, because the questions do not go away and are never adequately answered. The creation of myth, in other words, seems necessary to the human psyche and experience.

The Irish pantheon of gods is rather interesting when compared, say, to the Greeks. The Irish gods have little interaction with humans until about 500 BC, when they are defeated by humans, shrink, and retreat to the underworld in which they live today. Only one set of the ancient Irish gods could qualify as vicious and voracious and while the Irish gods can be capricious, they are not terribly punitive. They are quite lovely, physically, and they are inveterate lovers of story and music, qualities that are still central and necessary in Irish culture. Too,

no great world-ending apocalypse myth shapes the interactions of the Irish pantheon with each other or with their human contacts. It is perhaps these very characteristics that have allowed an Irish contact mythology to persist into modern times.

Storytelling, even in modern times, is essential and formative in Irish culture. Here, the author tells stories at the Grianán of Aileach, an ancient Irish ring fort at Inishowen (Inis Eoin) in Donegal. Photograph by Thomas McKnight

Historical Sources for Irish Origin and Myth Stories

It is important to understand that all Irish stories were passed down orally for nearly two thousand years before anyone wrote anything down, after which monks began to try to capture the whole oral tradition. Accordingly, more has been lost than it was possible to keep. Also, you want to think of these books more as collections of short stories, histories, poems, etc., much like the Norton Anthology books that we used in our undergraduate studies. Each of these books contains everything from history, to poems, to music, to stories, to law texts, to lots of marginalia and commentary from the many scribes who worked on them.

The Book of Drumm Snechtai. Eighth century. Unfortunately, while this book is referred to in later sources, the original manuscript was lost, most scholars say, to Viking raids.

Lebor Gabála Éirenn. Ninth through twelfth century. Translates as the "Book of the Conquest of Ireland." This is the purported history of the early settlement and conquest of Ireland and the races who came to Ireland and supplanted each other (see box below).

The Dindsenchas. 1150. Translates as the "History of Places"; this source uses both prose and meter to tell stories related to the places of Ireland. Many of these stories have attached themselves to places in ways that continue even into modern times.

The Leabhar na Huidre. Twelfth century. Translates as the "Book of the Dun Cow" because the book was supposedly written on the skin of St. Ciaran's favorite cow. The scribe of this book was Mael Muiri (it's amazing to actually know the name of the scribe) who was killed by robbers or Vikings in the church of Clonmacnoise in 1106.

Lebor Laignech. 1160. Translates as the "Book of Leinster." Originally, this book was probably called the *Lebor na Nuachongbála*, that is the "Book of Noghoval" because it was composed at the monastery of Oughaval in County Laois. Áed Ua Crimthainn might have been the primary scribe for this book, but there were certainly several people who worked on it. Crimthainn, however, was the Abbott of Terryglass in Tipperary and has signed the book and written a note stating that he compiled it by researching many earlier books. The "Táin bó Cúailgne" is contained in this book, the Irish epic of Cú Chulainn and the Brown Bull. (See my novel *Bright Sword of Ireland*).

Leabhar Buidhe Leacáin. 1391-1401. Translates as the "Yellow Book of Lecan." Among other gems, this book contains the full "Táin bó Cúailgne" and a life of my boyo St. Patrick (see my novel *I am of Irelaunde*). One of the strangest stories about this source is that a full version of the three-part *Wooing of Etain* from the *Yellow Book of Lecan* was found inside another book in a library in England. How it got separated from its original book is unclear. I love that the *Yellow Book of Lecan* also contains a tribute, by their names, to famous trees who were felled by a storm back in 665.

Leabhar Bhaile an Mhóta. Fifteenth century. Translates as the "Book of Ballymote." The likely primary scribe was Magnus O'Duignan, who came from a family of scribes. This book contains stories of Finn, but also the kingly instructions of Cormac Mac Art (see this book referenced in my novel *Daughter of Ireland*).

Leabhar Mac Carthaigh Riabhach. Fifteenth century. Translates as the "Book of Lismore." The lives of saints are contained in this tome, including, Patrick, Brigid, Ciaran, Brendan the Voyager, and Columcille, the exile to Iona. Fionn Mac Cumhaill stories are also written here.

The Ancient Races of Ireland (from the *Lebor Gabála;* or a glossary of our cast of mythical characters)

The People of Cesair. According to the *Lebor Gabála*, this entire race of people drowned in the Great Flood, with the exception of Cesair, a woman who survived and came to Ireland with her consort, Fintan, who was forced by the flood to shapeshift as a falcon, eagle, hawk, or salmon so that he could survive in air and water while the earth re-emerged. Scholars often say that this "race" was the attempt by the early monks to link themselves to Noah, the Ark, and the Biblical story of the Flood. Interestingly, however, the flood story exists in almost every culture's myths. What does this tell us? Simply, that something flooded—clearly something big. We always want to think of myth as popcorn. Just as there is always a hard kernel of corn beneath the fluff of popped corn, underneath all the fancies and frills of myth, there is a truth, an event, a central question. Something big flooded, but some people survived and repopulated or migrated. Thus, the people of Cesair. Note also the shapeshifting Fintan. Shapeshifting is a repeat motif— an archetype—throughout all of Irish myths, legends and folktales. The Irish clearly understood and valued transmogrification.

The Fomorians. We have read stories of these bad boys. Perhaps they were intended to explain evil, because they were a nasty bunch. They lived on Túr Rí, the Tower of the King, a rocky escarpment off the west coast of Ireland. They were piratical and terrifying. They demanded two-thirds of the crops, the cattle, and the firstborn children of the nearby residents of Ireland. They took slaves. Their secret weapon was a mythical giant with a deadly club and a killer eye in the middle of his forehead. Because of him, they were impossible to defeat until the arrival of the Tuatha de Danaan (see below).

The Partholon. According to the *Lebor Gabála*, these folks were craftsmen who lived in Ireland proper. They cleared four plains for planting, diverted nine rivers, created ten lakes. Here you see myth in its formative stages. How did this get here? Some race of ancient aliens must have put it here. As you are aware, such myth formation is still going on. Watch *Ancient Aliens* anyone? These Partholon also built the first guesthouse, brewed the first beer, brought gold and cattle to Ireland, and created the first legal system. They also tried to fight off the Fomorians. They sound like wonderful folks, but the *Lebor Gabála* tells us that the whole race died of a plague on the first of May, the date that would become the sacred Celtic feast of Beltaine.

The Nemedians. The Fomorians were particularly hard on these gentle folk, taking many of them as tribute slaves. Each year, on November 1, the Celtic feast of Samhain, they demanded tax tribute in the form of two-thirds of all the cattle, wheat, and children. At last, the Nemedians had to give up their landholds in Ireland and flee for the Continent to escape the Fomorians.

The Firbolg. Many scholars think this was a real race of migratory people who settled in western Connacht, perhaps the Gallic Belgae tribe (Celts of France). Some stories say that they were escaped slaves of the Greeks, while others say they arrived in Ireland accompanied by the Gauls of France and the Dumnonii of Britain, both Celtic tribes. They were often called "men of the bags," evidently from the habit of carrying materials in some kind of sling bag. In western Ireland, people claimed descent from the Firbolg for many generations.

The Tuatha de Danaan. These are the central race of Irish myth; stories persist about them to this day. Stories variously say that they came to Ireland from Greece, from Atlantis, from triangular cloud ships. Most of the myths have them landing on May 1, the sacred Celtic holiday of Beltaine. They were extraordinarily old, powerful, and learned. They did not grow old, they did not get sick, and if they died, that usually occurred because of war or combat. They are known as Ireland's "little people," but don't conflate them with leprechauns; those folkloric hoarders of gold are powerless and silly when compared to the Tuatha. The ancient gods of Irish mythology were almost all members of the Tuatha and were so pervasive that the pantheon of Celtic gods was found all throughout Europe, in England and in Ireland, where, even now, they are secretive and hidden, but not really gone.

Humans enter the world of the Other, (the Tuatha de Danaan) through portals. Boats headed west can take humans to Tir-nan-Og. Fairy mounds (Irish hills that are often topped with hawthorn trees) can open and take humans in. Passage graves and dolmens can open a door.

Water is also a portal in Irish myth. At Glencar Falls in County Leitrim (photo at left) Irish poet William Butler Yeats exhorted a human child to "Come away . . . with a fairy hand in hand."

In Irish myth, the child would disappear through the "waters and the wild," into the world of the Tuatha de Danaan, where he would live out his life, unaware that his human existence in the real world was over, because time passed differently in the world of the Others.

What would seem like three days to the human who entered the world of the sidhe would be three hundred years in earth time.

The Gods of Ireland's Pantheon

Ireland's Male Gods

- Balor One Eye
- Dagda
- Lugh
- Nuada
- Ogma
- Gobniu
- Dian Cecht
- Manannan Mac Lir
- Aengus Og
- Midir
- Lir

Ireland's Male Gods

Balor One Eye: Whereas all the other gods on our list are Tuatha de Danaan, Balor is a Fomorian, a giant possessed of a single killer eye. The Fomorians were pirates and raiders who lived on Tory Island (Tur Ri) off the west coast of Ireland. As many evil gods do, Balor eventually brings about his own demise. Balor believes a prophecy that he will be killed by his grandson, so he walls his only daughter Eithne up in a tower so that she can never marry or have children. However, Balor makes the mistake of stealing a magical cow from Cian of the Tuatha de Danaan. Cian disguises himself as a woman to sneak onto Tory Island to retrieve his cow and is given shelter in the tower by Eithne and her women. Naturally, Cian and Eithne fall in love, and she becomes pregnant with Lugh (see below). When Balor finds out, he swaddles Lugh and throws him into the sea, but the baby is rescued by Birog the druid, who gives the boy to his father, who has him fostered out in secret so that Balor can never find him. Eventually, it is indeed Lugh who kills his own grandfather at the Second Battle of Mag Tuired.

Dagda: Considered the "good" god of the Tuatha de Danaan, although this is not a comment on his character. Rather, he is a good provider. Dagda is an interesting god, because he is short, chubby, not at all good looking, and drags around a club so large that it requires wheels. However, he provides porridge from a bottomless cauldron and the club can restore life; these make him a strong paternal figure. He also plays the harp so beautifully that his music orders the seasons of each year. He can also play the three strains of music that control human behavior; the *geantraí* makes people to laugh, the *goiltaí* to weep and the *suantraí* to sleep. The harp is still the national symbol of Ireland. Dagda mates with the goddess Macha and with Boann, the river goddess. With Boann, he has a son, Aengus Og, who is the god of love.

Lugh: Lugh is such a powerful god figure that locations in Galicia, Spain (Lugones) and France (Lyon originally called Lugdunum) are named for Lugh. Some scholars claim him as the origin of the name London, although the Roman name was Londinium, so that probably carries more water. Lugh is the child of a Tuatha de Danaan father (Cian) and a Fomorian mother (Eithne). He is a light god, sometimes called the son of the sun. He has a number of nicknames, but the two most important are Lugh Lamfhada, (Lugh of the Long Arm) because he carries a long spear and is a true marksman with that spear and Lugh Samildánach (Lugh All Craftsman) because he is a carpenter, blacksmith, harper, poet, historian, sorcerer, swimmer, and warrior. The August harvest feast of Lughnasadh is named after Lugh. Lugh is the father of Cú Chulainn, so that makes Cú Chulainn a euhemerized figure (a man/god or god/man).

Nuada: Nuada is known as Argetlamh or Silver Hand, a story which constitutes one of the most fascinating battle stories in all of Irish mythology. He is the first king of the Tuatha de Danaan and possesses all the desirable attributes of kingship, as he is fair, just, honest and fights for his people. For years, I have told my students that I can't believe Marvel has not yet made a movie featuring Nuada Argetlamh. (See his story in the "Myths" section).

Ogma: Ogma is known as the "Honey Mouth" because he is the founder of language and a skilled poet. According to the myths, he also invented the Ogham language that is incised on stones all over Ireland, although many scholars date those stones to somewhere between the fourth and sixth centuries AD. However, Irish myth says that Ogham was originally incised on wooden sticks, some of which were used to predict the future (see my novel *Daughter of Ireland*). Because those sticks would not have survived archeologically, it is possible that the language is older.

Gobniu: Gobniu is a blacksmith god and he plays a role in crafting the Silver Arm for Nuada after he loses his arm in battle. Blacksmiths were absolutely essential in Celtic life because they crafted the metal rings for chariot wheels, the bits and bridlery for horses, but also the gorgeous chased metalwork of cups and cauldrons, torques, and bracelets. So they were both craftsmen and artists. In the story of how Cú Chulainn got his name, the opening feast is at the rath of a blacksmith. Blacksmiths were often wealthy, respected and powerful members of Celtic tribes.

Dian Cecht: Dian Cecht is the physician god of the Tuatha de Danaan and a tremendously skilled healer. He is father of many children. Through Cian, he is the paternal grandfather of Lugh. However, one of the key stories regarding Dian Cecht is his destruction of his own son Miach and the healing herb garden of his daughter Airmed after they regenerate a biological arm for Nuada. (See my novel *Song of Ireland*).

Manannan Mac Lir: Manannan is the god of the sea and he hides the undersea cities of the Tuatha de Danaan with mist and fog. His horse Aonbarr can gallop across the tops of the waves and his boat Scuabtinne needs no oars or sails to ply the seas. Most importantly Manannan guards the pathway to Tir-nan-Og, the Country of the Ever Young, the afterlife that is reached by sailing across the seas and into the West. One of the interesting stories about Manannan is his marriage to Fand, a woman of the sidhe who seduces Cú Chulainn while he is still married to his beloved wife Emer. (See my novel *Bright Sword of Ireland*).

Aengus Og: One of the most important things about Aengus is that he is the son of the Dagda and the goddess Boann, the goddess who is the archetype for Ireland's all-important river. Thus, archetypally, Aengus is a product of the union of the patriarch god with the land and water of Ireland. He is known as the god of love; in the legend of Dhiarmuid and Grainne, he is the guardian of Dhiarmuid and protects the young lovers as they flee from Fionn Mac Cumhaill.

Midir: In the pantheon of Irish gods, Midir is a minor figure, but he is the son of the Dagda and the primary figure in the complex and important story *The Wooing of Etain.*

Lir: Like Midir, Lir is a later and less important figure in the pantheon of Irish gods, but he is the father of the unfortunate children who are cursed into swan bodies in the famous story *The Children of Lir.*

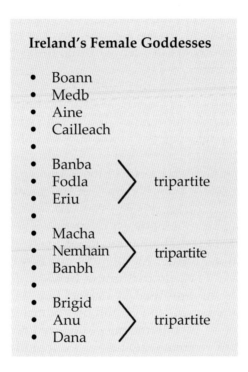

Ireland's Female Goddesses

Whereas Ireland's male gods are not triumvirate gods, the most powerful of Ireland's female goddesses are tripartite and in the case of Brig/Brigid, so powerful that syncretization (amalgamation of myth figures or myth/Christian figures) may have taken place. Many scholars say that the fact that Ireland had so many tripartite goddesses goes a long way toward explaining why Ireland Christianized so easily and with no bloodshed. The paradigm of three-part gods was already in place and clearly comprehended by the Irish.

Boann: Boann is the river goddess of Ireland's Boyne River. In Meath, the Boyne River is the center of Brúgh na Bóinne, the curving valley that contains Newgrange, Knowth, Dowth, and the great Hill of Tara. Myth has it that Boann created the river Boyne when her husband forbade her to do so (a behavior that is certainly consistent with Irish women). She approached the sacred well of Segais which was a source of wisdom because it was surrounded by nine sacred hazel trees. (The hazel nuts were eaten by the salmon who lived in the well and they became wise, which leads to our story of Fionn, Finegas, and the Salmon of Knowledge in our "Legends" section). Boann walked counterclockwise (called *tuathal)* around the well, which then overflowed and ran to the sea, but Boann was swept along with it and lost her life in the flood. Boann mated with the Dagda and they gave birth to Aengus Og, the god of love (see above).

Medb: Medb of Connacht is variously constructed as a war goddess or as the living/breathing human Queen of Connacht. While neo-pagans think of her as a goddess, it is possible that, like Cú Chulainn and Fionn, she is an euhemerized figure, a human queen of such staggering behaviors that mythology accrued around her. She was a woman (or a goddess) of voracious appetites for men, for possessions, for territory, and for the Brown Bull of Cooley, which started the entire war between Connacht and Ulster and resulted in Ireland's epic *Táin bó Cúailgne.* Some scholars say that she is the prototype for Shakespeare's Queen Mab in *Romeo and Juliet,* Mab of the play is a fairy figure, a charioteer, and thus a diminution of something that was once much larger.

Aine: You will not read much about Aine, but she is the goddess of midsummer and of wealth (wealth in ancient Ireland being reckoned by cattle and food) and therefore she is associated with warmth, sunlight and harvest. She must have been much recognized in ancient of days because numerous Irish places are named for her including Knockainey (Cnoc Áine) in Limerick, Dun Áine in Louth, and Tober Áine in Tyrone.

Cailleach: Cailleach simply means "hag." This old woman goddess brings winter onto the land and controls wind and storm and snow. She is the subject of a famous Irish verse "The Hag of Beara," translated by Lady Gregory during the Celtic Revival. In the poem, she laments her lost youth and beauty and is a figure of great pity. In myth and storytelling, the "crone" is an archetype. Always an old woman, she sometimes brings knowledge and wisdom, while at other times she is responsible for death and destruction. She is the third iteration of every female lifecycle in myth: maiden, mother, crone.

Banba, Fodla, Eriu: The gods of Ireland become truly interesting—long-lived and formidable for good or ill, when they take on tripartite form. The first of these tripartite groups have qualities that are less supernatural and more political. They are the sisters Banba, Fodla, and Eriu. Supposedly they took over as rulers of Ireland upon the death of three brothers (MacCuill, MacCecht, and MacGreine) who had been the rulers of the Tuatha de Danaan at their arrival in Ireland. Ireland (Eire) takes her name from Eriu. To learn more about them, see my novel *Song of Ireland.*

Macha, Banbh, Nemhain: This trilogy is known as **Morrigu.** Certainly, they constitute one of the most terrifying and persistent archetypes in all of Irish and even Celtic mythology. Again they are sisters, but not the kind of sisters you would ever want to have. Macha is the goddess of war. She is intelligent, powerful, dangerous, and quixotic. In various myths and legends, she appears to people as a beautiful woman, as a hag, as a wolf, an eel, a heifer. She is both a seductress and a punisher (see the story Macha Fleet Foot in the "Myths" section). You will meet her again in our "Legends" section because she dearly loves Cú Chulainn, the warrior of Ulster, but also gives him a terrible time when he does not do as she asks. Her other two "sisters" seem to be aspects of her dominance. Banbh is a war crow, a shapeshifter who lingers near battlefields and then takes carrion-eater form when the war is over. Nemhain, the third sister of the set is the personification of Chaos, of the term the "fog of war." She causes confusion, disorientation, mist, fog, anything that will cause humans to battle, fail, and die.

This trilogy is so powerful that they show up as the Three Weird Sisters in *Macbeth*, predictors of glory who instead sow chaos and confusion. Later, in the Arthurian epics, the tripartite nature of the Morrigu becomes conflated into the single figure of Morgan le Fay, who sows chaos for the whole of Camelot with dark magic, eventually causing the death of King Arthur at the hand of his own illegitimate and incestuous son Mordred.

You might be tempted to think of Morrigu as analogous to the Three Fates of Greek myth, but Morrigu does not determine a person's fate or the length of their life. She is not a proactive archetype. Rather, Morrigu interferes at every turn and does so, almost always, for selfish and destructive purposes. Morrigu is an active presence in all Irish myths and legends.

Brigid/Anu/Dana: This is the most powerful tripartite archetype in all of Irish myth and yet it is the most difficult to define. Some scholars think that it is all the same person. Others see it through a mother/daughter lens while almost all agree that it became a syncretized Christian archetype, who was then also a real person and a saint. Confused yet?

Anu and Dana (or Danu)—all three evidently the same name—is the mother goddess of Celtic myth. Or at least, linguistically, it would seem so because the magical people who are known, variously, as the Others, the sidhe, the little people, the Good Folk or Good People or the Fair Folk are actually the Tuatha de Danaan or Tribe of the Goddess Danu. There are some place names in Ireland that are associated with her, for example, the Paps of Anu in County Kerry, but beyond all of this, there is no lineage and there are no stories associated with this figure. Most scholars will say that the tripartite nature of the Brigid goddess probably has nothing whatsoever to do with Anu/Dana.

Brigid herself, (Brigit/Brig/Brid) however, is another story. Brigid is the single most powerful female deity figure in Irish mythology and she is the patroness of all the creative forces in the world: fire, childbirth, ewes, poetry, wisdom, holy wells, healing, blacksmithing. In fact, the triple nature of the Brigid may come not from the Anu or Dana connection, but from the fact that myths refer to three aspects of the Brigid: the Wise, the Healer and the Smith. In the myths, she is the daughter of the Dagda.

Some scholars believe that the pagan goddess Brigid became syncretized with St. Brigid of Kildare; we will talk more about that in our "Legends" sections.

Legends

Part II: Legends: Heroes in Love and War

Legends: Whooo Wants to Know More?

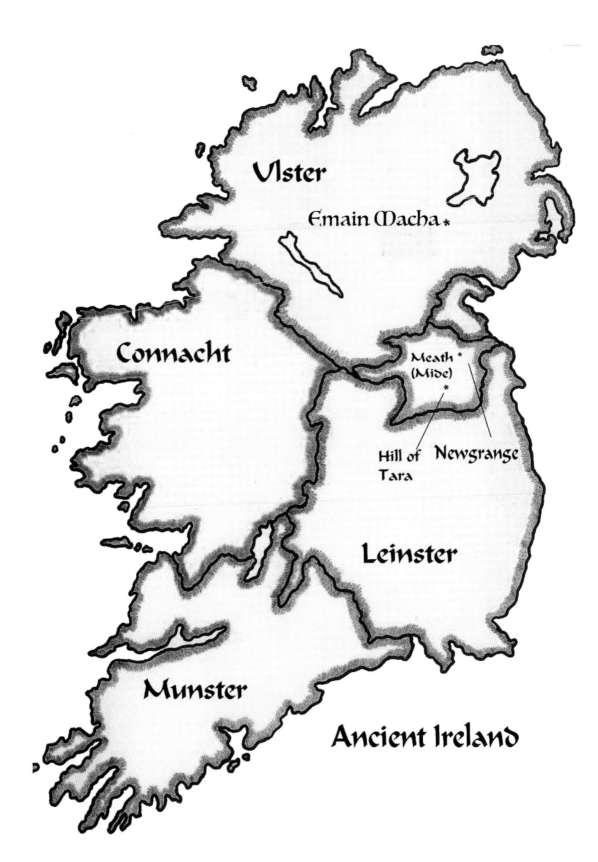

Ulster

Emain Macha *

Connacht

Meath *
(Mide)
*

Hill of
Tara

Newgrange

Leinster

Munster

Ancient Ireland

Chapter 1

The *Táin bó Cúailgne:* Legends of the Ulster Cycle

The *Táin Bó Cúailgne* is Ireland's *Iliad* and *Odyssey*. It is the epic story of a foolish war over a bull that is nonetheless bloody, heartbreaking, and full of ancient life.

It contains some thirty sections within the epic, and many of those are broken into subsections telling more tales. It is also surrounded by *remscéla* or border stories that function as prologue and epilogue tales. The full tale is ten times the length of what we have here. The entire tale could never be read in one sitting because the reader must stop and absorb, think, translate, and locate stories geographically.

Stylistically, the *Táin* is a treasure trove of place names and character names, of specific information on weaponry, transportation, and garb. Linguistically, it is a mix of prose and high chanted poetry.

A facsimile page of the Tain *from the translation of the epic by Professor Joseph Dunn on Project Gutenberg.* Open-source materials.

For our purposes as American readers, and for the length limitations of this book, we are introducing the *Tain* here with eight short tales. These stories follow the arc of the *Tain* and give its flavor, while focusing heavily on the boy Cú Chulainn, on the warrior he became, and on the women, friends, and family who knew him and loved him.

He was, in all likelihood, a real person, who fought and died bravely in Ulster in a long-ago and violent time.

Setanta and the Blacksmith's Hound

Down the road, the boy Setanta ran, his chubby legs pumping, his wide arms raising the hurley stick every few steps, slicing at the air so hard that the wind made a whooshing sound as it parted over his stick. Every little while, he would catch up to his *sliotar,* the hard leather ball filled with animal hair and ringed with bronze. This happened less often than his mother expected it to, because each time Setanta hit the *sliotar* with the hurley, it seemed to travel further and further down the long road.

Deichtine smiled with motherly pride and reached for her husband's hand where he rode beside her on their matching roan horses.

How lucky they had been. For years, Deichtine had been unable to bear a child, but then, at last, their dear son came along. At seven, he was the mirror-glass of his father, though neither of them knew it. Setanta was short with chubby legs and broad muscular arms, just like her husband Súaldem. His face was wide, due to the bulbous nose that occupied the center of his face, again the mirror of Súaldem. He would never be considered the handsomest boy in Eire, no, but he was funny, gifted with poetry and song, skilled at every athletic feat, in demand on the hurley team in their little rath, a hard worker who never tired of laboring by his father's side.

Oh, they were lucky and proud.

She glanced down the long road to see that he had gone too far before them. She was about to call out to him, to tell him to stay closer to her and Súaldem when he threw his *sliotar* in the air and brought his hurley up in his hands.

Deichtine silenced herself. No mother of a seven-year-old boy would interrupt him when he was batting his *sliotar* down the road!

Not without paying the price of sullenness or rolling eyes. Besides, they were almost at the great rath of Culann the Smith. Ahead, Deichtine could see the palisaded walls at the crest of a little hill by the river.

"It really is splendid," she whispered to Súaldem, who nodded.

"It will be an epic feast," he agreed.

And then their boy made contact with his *sliotar*. First there was the solid *thunk* of wood and leather and then the rush of displaced wind. The ball rocketed down the tree-lined roadway.

Setanta leapt in the air with delight at the strong, straight hit.

And then came the yelp.

"He must die!"

Culann the Smith roared over the heads of the crowd from his place seated in the dust. In his arms he cradled his great mastiff, the dog he had raised from a whelp, the beloved dog he had trained to guard his rath. In his hand he held a dripping, saliva-covered *sliotar*, a leather ball with a bronze band.

Again he roared, "The boy Setanta must die."

Deichtine made to step forward. She was, after all, the daughter of a druid, the sister of King Conor Mac Nessa of Ireland. No one was going to threaten her son over a dead dog.

Setanta himself had dropped to his knees in the dirt, his hand reaching toward the dead dog, his face contorted in sorrow.

Culann leapt to his feet, holding his hand out to one of his warriors who threw him a short sword. He was bringing it down toward the neck of her son when everything changed.

What happened Deichtine could not say.

Setanta came to his feet in one fluid motion. For a moment, in the bright sunlight, he was not her burly boy, short and squat on stubby legs. He was seven feet tall—maybe even nine. His red-gold hair flowed down to the center of his back. He exhaled a long breath and Deichtine could have sworn she saw fire.

For a moment, for a strange, long moment, Deichtine was troubled by a memory—a memory of firelight and a man in a nimbus of golden light.

But the moment passed, and before her, Deichtine once more

saw her boy—her awkward, roly-poly boy. He was standing before Culann the Smith, his head bowed. Yet, somehow, he was holding the blacksmith's sword. Culann himself looked surprised, staring up at his empty hand with a look of complete confusion.

Setanta spoke. "I have done this terrible thing, great smith. My heart sorrows for your beloved dog and for you. I must make reparations. I do not wish to pay with my life. I wish to pay for the life of your dog. For one year, I will be your dog. I will live in the dwelling of your dog. I will guard your rath with my life. That year will give you time to choose a new dog and train him in your service. At the end of that year, if I have not served you as well as this great guardian, I will offer you my life. Will that serve, great smith?"

Deichtine and Súaldem stared at their son. He spoke to them most of the time in grunts and laughter. He surely gave no speeches. Yet this was a speech as old and wise as all of Eire.

Culann the Smith pondered for a moment.

"Come," he said. "I will show you to your dwelling."

The dwelling was a doghouse.

Setanta nodded when he saw it and lifted his shoulder in a shrug.

The small stone hut was just outside the gate at the top of the causeway leading into the rath. On the opposite side, a second doghouse housed a great wolfhound who growled in the boy's direction as if he already knew the crime that had been committed.

"Are you still willing to serve this sentence?" the smith asked. His anger had cooled on the heels of the boy's speech. By the gods, Deichtine and Súaldem had raised a young man of honor.

As if to prove it, the boy cried out to the assembled company, "It will be my duty and my honor."

Culann handed him his hurling stick. "This must serve as your spear, boy. You can have no other, for this became your weapon, though I can see that it was weapon unintended."

And so began Setanta's year of penitence. He lined the inside of his little hut with wolf pelts and warm wools, doing the same for the opposite dog whom Culann had named Mac Tire, or wolf, a name Setanta thought was disrespectful to the nature of the dog, whom he took to calling Cróga, which meant brave.

Together, they challenged every comer—bards who arrived with stories, brehons who arrived to adjudicate a case, even King Conor Mac Nessa, Setanta's own uncle, whose face quirked when the boy cried, "Stand fast and declare yourself, for I am Culann's dog."

"Good bark, boy," Conor said in response, but when his nephew still did not yield the doorway, still stood with his hurling stick crossed over his chest like a spear, the king relented. He put his hand over his mouth to keep from laughing and spoke to Setanta in a whisper, "I am the high king of Ulster, come to see the smith about a chariot wheel," at which point his nephew stood aside.

Once, in the dark of a moonless night, there was a cattle raid. A distant tribe from Connacht came through the darkness, seeking to steal the fabled cows of the wealthy smith. Both Cróga and Setanta heard them long before they arrived and they were standing amid the sleeping herd, silent as pillars when the thieves entered the pasture. The dog barked once and the boy said nothing, but afterwards, in the midst of their own tribe, the would-be thieves swore that the man who drove them away was nine feet tall, that he stood atop a hurling stick, that he breathed fire.

In Ulster, the people began to tell stories. The boy who could talk with his companion dog. The boy of seven years who was nine feet tall. The boy whose fiery visage frightened every would-be invader.

And then came the night of the she-wolf.

Setanta had been catching small birds, pinging them from the air with his slingshot. He had skewered them over his fire and one by one he and Cróga ate the dripping meat. That was when the she-wolf appeared at the bottom of the causeway.

The night was a good one, full moon and myriad stars, so Setanta could see her clearly from the top of the causeway as she began her careful ascent. He did not fear wolves. They were intelligent and silent, and he admired their ability to appear at the wood's line with no notice whatsoever. This one, however, had deep red fur, red as the hide of a fox.

Setanta sniffed the air.

Cróga stopped eating and growled deep in his throat. As a wolfhound, he knew his job with this one, and he stood to his full height, all the springy, gray hair along his back shivering to attention.

And then the moonlight hit the eyes of the wolf. They were black, abyssal. They reflected no light. That is when Setanta came to his feet.

"You are not a wolf," he said aloud. The sound of his voice cascaded down the high causeway. He signaled to Cróga to retreat to his own hut; the wolfhound did so with a low whine.

Still, the she-wolf advanced the causeway, wind ruffling her fur. At last, she was close enough that Setanta could see his fire reflected in her eyes.

Setanta shifted his hurling stick across his body and gave his usual greeting. "State your purpose at the causeway of Culann the Smith."

The wolf tipped her head in his direction. The fire rippled and shifted, sparks ascending skyward, but Setanta did not allow himself to look away from the eyes of the wolf. Even so, he did not see the shape-shift, so invisibly did it occur. First there was a wolf, then there was a woman, beautiful and lissome, black hair cascading all around her. Still, the fathomless black eyes.

"My purpose is you," she said.

The boy could feel his heart hammering in his chest, but he kept his tongue. Best to listen. Best to learn what could be learned.

She smiled at his silence. Even white teeth. Sharp canines.

"I am hearing stories," she said, softly. "They tell me that the sleeping war-boy awakes."

This made no sense to Setanta at all. What war-boy? He was a boy dog, guarding the rath of a smith.

"I am doing my job," he said. "I am making reparations to the smith. I have not been asked to go to war, but if he asks me, I will go."

Privately, he had already thought that it would be much less boring than sitting here in this doghouse. He had thought, for a moment, that he might say something to his uncle when he arrived for his chariot wheel, but he had set that thought aside. He owed a debt of one year, which was almost over; he would fulfill his debt.

While he thought these thoughts, the woman watched him. "You do not seem surprised that I am not a wolf."

Setanta shrugged. "All things that have been created are from the same dust. That dust takes many forms. Have we not always known this?"

She tilted her head and regarded him. "We have," she said. "You have a good understanding of that malleability for a boy of seven. You are wise beyond your youth."

"Thank you." He had no real idea what she was talking about, but he knew to be polite.

Now she laughed aloud. "But you are resisting your other knowledge, boy. The knowledge of your own malleability. We must awake that sleeper."

She lifted her hand, and suddenly crows flew at him from every direction. Raucous and wheeling, black as the night, they dived at his head, swept toward his feet. Anger raced through the boy. He raised his hurling stick to fend them off, each crow a *sliotar*, batted away through the darkness, though more and more arrived.

The boy roared. He heard the sound issue from his mouth. He roared again. Flames encircled his head, and the crows were forced to dive for his chest. One impaled its beak into the skin above his heart. Again, he roared. Now, he swept his arm in great circles, battering crows in every direction. His arms reached longer than they had ever reached. They windmilled unceasingly, huge with muscle, powerful. He leapt onto the roof of his doghouse, his back against the wall of the fortress. He stood on one foot and grasped his hurley with his free leg. While his arms beat off the attacking crows, he aimed his hurley at the source of his trouble, the head of the woman.

He flung it with his foot.

It spun outward toward her, its momentum faster and wider than his slingshot, than any spear he had ever used for practice. It connected with her head and knocked her into the dust. For a moment, she vanished entirely. The boy, still standing on one leg, stared at the dust where she had been, where now only his hurley remained. But the crows had stopped attacking.

"At last. There you are." He spun to his left, to see her standing atop Cróga's doghouse, unharmed, her nearly transparent dress the color of the moon.

He felt his jaw drop. He realized suddenly that he was still standing on one leg and he set it down with a conscious effort. He realized that he was so tall that he could see over the top of the wooden palisade that surrounded the rath. Inside, people had emerged from their huts, called forth by the racket. They stared up at him in astonishment. He put both hands on the top of the palisades so that they might think he was holding on, raising his head above the walls.

"Crows!" he shouted down at them. "I think they're gone now."

He bent in half from his knees and scrunched low, hoping that they would think he had dropped his hold. Even in that position, his head reached almost to the top of the wall. From his squat position, he turned to face the woman. She was holding his hurley in her hand, and she looked exceedingly pleased with herself. She tossed it to him, and he caught it mid-air. From within the doghouse, he heard the low, terrified whine of Cróga.

"My friend is brave," he said in a whisper. "But he does not understand the likes of you. Withdraw from him."

She looked down at the doghouse and up at him and smiled. The next moment she was standing in the path. He leapt from his own doghouse and approached her. He towered over her, and she had to bend backwards to look up at him.

"Beautiful boy," she said, smiling up at him. "We have waited since the first night of the crows. It has been a very long wait."

"What has happened here?" he whispered.

"You have come forth," she replied. "This was in you always."

"That is not possible."

"You are your father's son."

"My father has no such abilities."

"Ah but your true father does. You must ask your mother. Ask her about the night of the chariot crows."

Something terrible moved in Setanta now. He breathed in her direction, a hot breath, a breath of fire. "Do you impugn my mother?"

She raised her palm. "No. What we did was necessary. We will stand with you. We of Morrigu. You will be my war dog. But do not reject me, Hound. Do not ever reject me. For my revenge would be a terrible thing."

Setanta stood very tall over her.

"You call yourself Morrigu. I have heard these tales. Know that I will reject all that is evil, dark one. I will move only within my honor. This will be my way."

She sighed. "Again, your father's son. Your honor will be your downfall."

"Then so it shall be. You cannot take it from me."

He came to, seated before his fire, Cróga beside him, blackened birds turning on the spit.

So, it had been a dream? Only a dream?

Still, he thought, still, he might ask his mother about the night of the chariot crows.

But that thought fled in the morning when he awoke to horns and drums, to the fact that his year of penitence had ended. His parents and his uncle came for a great feast in his honor and the poet of Culann the Smith proclaimed a *rosc* of poetry in his honor, inflating his dog deeds to the level of legend.

"What you have done was brave and sacrificial," the poet proclaimed. "You have defended us well. You have given our chief time to train our new defenders."

Now Culann the Smith brought forth two gigantic mastiffs, who flanked him on either side. "Ask for anything," the smith called, "and that gift will be yours."

Setanta searched the room, until at last his eyes lighted on Crogá, stretched out on the floor beneath the feet of his uncle, the king of Ulster. Setanta held out his hand. The wolfhound leapt to his feet and ran to the boy, his head coming almost to the shoulder of Setanta.

"I ask that my friend and fellow guard be allowed to accompany me on my journey."

"Done!" cried the smith, who had clearly anticipated this request, as evidenced by his matched pair of new dogs.

"And now we will give you a new name. A name that befits the honor and strength with which you have defended us. May all of Eire speak of your deeds for all of time! For from this day forward, you will be known as Cú Chulainn, the Hound of Ulster!"

The *Riastradh* of Cú Chulainn

Called the "warp-spasm" or the "war-spasm," Cú Chulainn's transformation is his Iron Man suit, his Superman cape. In his warp, he grows from five feet tall to nine feet tall. From this great height, he can see over treetops and across water. His head spins 360 degrees on his neck, like an owl. One of his eyes retreats into his skull, but the other bulges forward. He breathes fire or spurts blood from his forehead or both. He is now capable of the "salmon-leap," a giant leap that can take him to the middle of rivers, up cliffs or over chasms. Most dangerous is his "*gae bulga*," his great spear, which is barbed at the tips with fishhooks that open inside his intended target. He never misses with this weapon, because he stands on one leg and throws it with his foot, keeping his arms free for other weapons. Cú Chulainn has a hard time coming out of these spasms as you will see in the story *The Lake of Women*.

Cú Chulainn and the Lake of Women

"Y'ere goin' ta haf ta stop the lad!"

"He's a twelve-year-old boy." Conor Mac Nessa, the high king of Ulster waved his hand in the direction of his servant Conrí. "You're making too much of this. He's just a boy feeling his oats. Remember that he was only recently named the Hound of Ulster."

"*Ard Rí,*" said the old man, who was past the point where he felt any deference to kings, "beggin' y'er pardon, but this is no wee laddie beyond. He's been out waging battle on our own men all the day long. He's nine feet tall. His hair is on fire. He's a monster screamin' mayhem. Will ye not come see for yerself?"

Conor sighed. He rose from his chair and drew his cloak around him. "Where is he then?"

"Down by the lake. Thundering around it in his chariot."

Conor made for the door. He actually was curious about the boy's hair being on fire.

Beside the lake, the charioteer Laeg Mac Riangabra was driving the chariot around the lake at breakneck speed. Rope thin and hard to rattle, today Laeg had a look on his face that resembled the startled creature beside him.

"Is that . . . a buck?"

"Tis," said the king's retainer. "The lad captured it and threw it in the chariot with Laeg. Laeg has been driving him around the lake to keep him from causing mayhem among the people. The boy keeps shouting that he needs to kill something."

Beside Laeg in the chariot, a stag of eight tines barely kept his balance, tipping side to side like a poorly anchored statue.

Conor Mac Nessa was a man used to getting his way. He stood to the side as the chariot passed and looked up at his nephew, who was standing on the bar between the horses.

"Come down, Cú Chulainn," he called up to his nephew, who was indeed nine feet tall, whose hair was indeed standing up on end, the tips on fire.

"Nay," the boy thundered. "Bring me something I can kill!!"

The people began to gather now, all of them agape. Conor's chief wife, Mugain, sidled up beside him. "What has happened to him, husband?"

Conor had no idea; he found the question irritating because he had no answer for it. He gestured toward his servant Conrí.

"Ask old Conrí here. King of Hounds. He seems to know everything."

Conrí rolled his eyes. Wasn't it just like a king to pass the reins? He turned toward Conor's wife. "It's that woman what did it I'd say. That cursed dark woman. She is forever meddling with Ulster, is she not now?"

Conor's wife tipped her head. "Are you speaking of Macha of Morrigu?"

Conrí made the sign against the evil and waved it above his head. "Dinna speak the name."

By now the chariot had thundered all the way around the lake and was approaching the turn. The buck was standing on its hind legs, forelegs on the front of the chariot, eyes wild with terror. It looked like a second charioteer and Conor laughed out loud.

Mugain looked at him in disgust. "You won't think it's funny if that monster comes down among us." She clapped her hands. "Ladies! Ladies! Join me now."

When all the women had surrounded her and when the chariot had thundered toward the back of the lake, she spoke to the assembled women. "Despite his fearsome size, this is a twelve-year-old boy. We all know what is most terrifying to a boy that age, do we not?"

General laughter erupted.

"Good then," Mugain said. "We will array ourselves down to the water, so that Laeg will know to drive into the lake."

When the chariot wheeled back toward them, more than a hundred women were arrayed in its path.

Laeg began to turn the wheel just as the boy began to roar, but Mugain knew exactly what must be done.

"Disrobe now!" she called aloud.

Cloaks and tunics flew into the air and settled down to the ground around hundreds of naked women.

The face of the giant boy reddened right to the roots of his flaming hair. He lifted his giant hands and covered his face. It was enough, just enough. Laeg halted the chariot when the horses were up to their knees in the water. The buck leapt from the stopped vehicle and ran for the woods. And the men of Ulster, hundreds of them, tackled the boy and tumbled him into the water.

The water began to steam and hiss, and the boy stood up, bedraggled but still nine feet tall. So, the women walked into the water and approached him. He backed away, stumbled over stones and sank beneath the icy surface. And there he stayed, the water steaming above his head for a long few minutes. When at last he sputtered to the surface, he was again the pudgy twelve-year-old boy that the whole tribe knew and loved.

Surrounded by naked women, still hiding his face behind his palms—something the grown men of Ulster were not doing at all—he kept murmuring his apologies.

He refused to leave the water until all of the women had departed, wrapping themselves in their cloaks. At last, it was only Cú Chulainn, Conor, and Conrí standing in the water while Laeg Mac Riangabra backed the chariot out onto the track and dried the legs of the horses with his own tunic.

"All right now," said Conor.

Conrí shook his head. Why did people assume that kings possessed wisdom? "Are ye all right then laddie?" Conrí asked the boy.

Cú Chulainn shook his head. "I shamed myself in front of the women of the tribe. I will never be able to look at them again."

Conrí nudged the silent king in the ribs. Conor cleared his throat.

"Well," he began. "They were giving you an important lesson, nephew. A lesson about control. It seems to me that you have been given a gift here. A war gift. But you have to learn to control it."

Conrí closed his eyes. Of all the subjects for Conor to address, women? Women? King Conor Mac Nessa had no control when it came to women. Conrí wisely held his tongue. The boy nodded.

"Thank you, Uncle," the boy said seriously. "You are wise, as always. I will learn to control this . . . transformation. And I will use it to protect the women of Ulster."

"Good lad," said Conor Mac Nessa, clapping his nephew on the shoulder. "There is always much to be learned from the women of Ulster."

Behind the king's back, Conrí rolled his eyes.

The Roles of Women in Ancient Ireland

Most people assume that women were relegated to the typical female medieval roles in Ireland, but Irish society was in no way similar to British or European society. Irish women had much more autonomy.

Irish women were sometimes queens, as you will see when we meet Medb of Connacht. They could be warriors, charioteers, druids, physicians, lawyers, and judges (brehons or britheamh). They owned land and property. They could make the choice of a husband or reject a suitor. They were not the property of either their fathers or their husbands.

Marriage was very unusual in ancient Ireland. For one thing, there were *nine* different forms of marriage under Irish law! Some were centered around property, as there were marriages where both parties were equal and marriages where either the woman or man owned more property.

But Brehon law also provided for cohabitation, elopement, and even marriage between two people who were not of sound mind!

Women also owned their own land and property; divorce was legal, and women kept their property upon divorce. Too, no child from any of these arrangements was considered illegitimate, and the law carefully set out who was responsible for the care and raising of all children.

One of the most unusual marriage arrangements in ancient Ireland was that a man of high standing, such as a chief, could have multiple wives, but his primary wife—called his *cét muinter*—had three days in which to lament his choice by hitting the new wife, pulling her hair, and generally railing against that choice, after which the women had to find a way to get along.

There are almost no cases of women taking multiple husbands, one, presumably, being trouble enough.

The Pillow Talk of Medb and Ailill

Ailill, husband and consort of Queen Medb of Connacht, cringed. Side by side on the wolf pelts covering the bed, Medb had carefully set two candlesticks of chased silver, one by his pillow and one by hers.

So, it was to be a counting night.

Ailill loathed the counting, but he had brought it on himself; this he knew.

Had he not made the mistake the very night before when they were pillowed and warm, made the mistake of teasing her that she was lucky to have married him, wealthy as he was, son of the king of Leinster and with such prowess between the sheets.

It never did to diminish Medb's power. It never did.

He sighed as she entered the room.

With her were her servants, bearing platters and cups, woven cloaks and elaborate sandals, daggers and spears, bracelets and diadems and torques of hammered gold.

Medb smiled sweetly at him. "Let us see who is lucky, shall we?" she said. "Let us see who possesses more wealth?"

Oh, the counting went on into the small hours. She counted the linens and the woolen bedclothes, wall hangings, and the pillows. In all things, they were equal, just as they had been when last they counted their wealth.

Once they had finished the household goods, Medb moved on to the animals. The sheep were counted, the pigs, and the goats. Ailill thought that Medb would have counted every stalk of wheat if she could have done. Wisely, he did not voice this thought.

And then, at last, they came to the cattle—milch cows and meat, heifers and calves—and finally, the bulls.

Equal again on every beast.

Every beast but one.

"Well," said Medb. The sun had begun to rise by now and they were staring at the enclosure that held Ailill's proudest possession—Finnbennach, the magical white bull.

"Remember wife," he said at last. "You gave him to me, this big fellow."

"I gave him to you expecting that you would return the gift. A magical bull for a magical bull. I am the queen of Connacht, the ruler at Cruachan Ai. I deserve no less."

"You gave him to me because he was so dangerous, because he would not let you near him."

"Another male who does not respect women."

"Wife, were there another magical bull in all of Connacht, I would give him to you."

Medb's eyes glittered. She clapped her hands. "Call Mac Roth!" she cried to her servants. "Bring him to me."

Inwardly Ailill cringed. Mac Roth was Medb's man of all things. Mac Roth knew everyone. He knew everywhere. He knew everything. Ailill could feel his purse lightening even as they awaited the arrival of her herald.

When Mac Roth arrived, Ailill shook his head. How did such a strange little man ever become Medb's right hand? He was short and bald, thin and stoop-shouldered. His cloak was drawn about him wrong, fastened to slip continually from his shoulders. No matter what anyone asked him, his first reaction was to look confused. He did that now.

"Mac Roth," Medb said in her most commanding tones. "Where in all of Connacht is there a magical bull? A bull with the prowess and power of my consort's Finnbennach."

Ailill bit his lip. Consort, was it? Well, she was well displeased now.

Mac Roth looked befuddled, something that he never really was, yet Medb stood over him and kissed the top of his head with true affection. She never angered at Mac Roth.

"Ah, my queen," Mac Roth intoned, shaking his head like a sad dog. "In all of Connacht, no bull possesses the prowess of Finnbennach."

Ailill could see her anger rising. Her beautiful, white neck spackled; her cheeks grew red. But before she could say a word, Mac Roth raised a finger.

"However," he said.

How did the man know exactly how to time his pronouncements?

"In Ulster, there is a bull mightier still than Finnbennach, mightier than any bull in all of Eire. Donn Cúailgne, they call him, the pride of Dáire the Boaire. The Brown Bull of Cooley. From him, calves have filled the fields of Ulster!"

Medb clapped her hands.

"Then that is the bull that I must have."

"Dáire would never sell him my queen. He is the source of all Dáire's wealth."

Medb thought on this for a few moments and then smiled. "Fine. We will rent him for a year, and he will sire calves. At the end of that year, we will count the calves of Finnbennach and the calves of Donn Cúailgne. The winner will possess the most calves. And then we will return Donn Cúailgne. . . . And kill Finnbennach. And so will end this competition."

The whole company was silent. No Irish man or woman worth the salt would ever kill a breeding bull. Yet, all of them knew that Medb would do just that. And no one said a word.

"Gather the lawyers," she said cheerfully. "Go to Dáire and put together a contract. Mac Roth, you have solved this beautifully, as always."

Whether Mac Roth thought the solution worthy, Ailill would never know, for Medb had pressed him into a hug between her ample, white breasts where he was not capable of saying a single word.

"So," said Dáire, when the feast was finished and the men were raising their mead cups. "Why are we here, Mac Roth? And why so many lawyers?" For Mac Roth had traveled with a retinue of nine.

Mac Roth sighed.

"Back to home, the two of them have had a disagreement. A donnybrook of staggering proportions. And all of it over a bull."

"Ah," said Dáire, who saw immediately where this was going. "I will nae sell the lad."

"No," said Mac Roth. "She wishes only to rent him for a year."

"She will put him to sire."

"Aye. Again, and yet again."

"And what will she give me for the purpose?"

"Gold, of course, and generous. Pasturage. A dozen heifers."

Dáire nodded slowly. "Well, it all sounds fair. Have the lawyers draw it up."

No sooner had the words left his mouth than one of the lawyers drew forth a wordy vellum and Dáire made his mark.

"Now," he said, "let's feast the night away, drink mead, and tell some tales."

The tales were the undoing of the contract. For was it not one of Medb's own soldiers who said to one of Dáire's guards, "Ah now. 'Tis good yer man signed on. For had he not, Medb would have mustered her army and taken the great bull from him."

"No one could take that bull from Dáire," said the guard, who promptly told his master, who threw the contract into the dancing fire, then threw Mac Roth and all the lawyers out onto the road.

So, the foolish war began. For Medb wanted the bull. And she wanted to win the counting. And she mustered her army and prepared them to enter Ulster.

Legendary American breeding bull Legacy. Photo courtesy of Mike and Cindy McPhee.

Cattle in Ancient Ireland

Cattle were the economic engine of ancient Ireland. A *"boaire"* or cattle man who was rich in cattle was rich indeed. Cattle provided milk, meat, leather, and future cattle, i.e. many of the basic necessities of ancient life.

Cattle were purified through sacred smoke during Beltaine (May 1) rituals, guarded carefully, and often raided, so there was an extensive system of laws for making reparations when cattle were stolen or killed.

In Irish myth, cattle are often referred to as "magical." In the story of Cian and Eithne, Glas Gaibheann is a milk cow. Her magic is that she gives milk unceasingly. Finnbennach and Donn Cúailgne are bulls. The magic there means being good sires.

Lawyers in Ancient Ireland

You may have thought that it was an anachronism when Medb tells her herald Mac Roth to gather the lawyers, but no. At one point during the reign of Conor Mac Nessa in Ulster there were actually more than 1200 lawyers. In fact, during this period, some people took to just declaring themselves to be lawyers and they developed a secret "lawyer's language." If you've ever worked with or for a lawyer and tried to translate their handwriting, this will not surprise you at all.

In order to standardize the practice of law, King Conor Mac Nessa authorized a law school. Legal training lasted for twelve years and culminated in a standing exam before a panel of judges, much the same as now. In ancient times, law was practiced by memory, so a good brehon (breitheamh) knew all of the precedent cases of the same type for every case going back hundreds of years.

This body of laws was called the *Féineachas* (basically "law of the free farmers"). Cases were heard four times a year at the four major festivals, when everyone would travel either to Emain Macha in Ulster, or later to Tara in Meath. There, judges would hear cases and make rulings; many of these cases were written down in the Middle Ages and are still extant. Many of those rulings are from women judges.

Rulings arose from a system of recompense called "erics." These erics were honor payments; they covered everything from beekeeping, in which *bumbog* or bees could be accused of trespassing and thus send their keepers to court or to breaking the nail of a harper, which required paying the harper until the nail grew back, to marriage, hospitality, land ownership, cattle theft, murder, and mayhem.

A person who had no money for a lawyer could "sue" by carrying on a hunger fast outside the door of the person who had wronged them. This was the tradition that Bobby Sands and the hunger strikers were following in the Maze prison in the 1980s.

Eventually, these laws were compiled as the *Seanchus Mór* or Big Ancient Tradition. Legend has it that St. Patrick was given the responsibility for this compilation.

For more on this subject, including some of the most fascinating ancient laws, see our book *The Story We Carry in our Bones: Irish History for Americans*.

The burial cairn of Medb of Connacht at Knocknarea. While it actually is a burial cairn, there is no proof that Medb is buried within.

Medb: Myth and History

Medb ruled from Cruachan Ai, now known at Rathcrogran. This is a real place in County Roscommon, not far from the village of Tulsk, and you can visit this archeological center. It is a massive complex which includes burial mounds like those at Newgrange and circles that would certainly have held great forts. It was likely the headquarters of the Connachta in ancient times and thus, would have been used for great fairs with games, genealogy, law cases, and more.

Queen Medb (sometimes spelled Maeve) is likely a syncretization (see "Legends: Whooo Wants to Know More"), i.e. a real historical person who also became conflated with a more ancient Celtic goddess. Scholars wage their own wars over this contention, some seeing her as wholly human, others as wholly mythical. In her human guise, she is sexually voracious, demanding, and utterly ruthless. Medb kills her own sister Clothu, who was carrying the child of Conor Mac Nessa, so that Medb can take the throne of Connacht. She lusts after Cú Chulainn but plots his death to get the Brown Bull. Eventually, Medb is killed by her sister's son Furbaide, who hits her in the forehead with a piece of hard cheese released from his slingshot. Death by cheese.

She is supposedly buried in the high cairn of Knocknarea, above.

In her divine or otherworldly guise, she is looked upon as the goddess of war, intoxication, and fertility. Her name is associated with mead; her urine creates lakes and rivers, and trees near magical wells are called Bile Medb.

The Auction of Finnabair

She sold me. My mother. Like a broodmare, like a breeding cow. Like the cursed bull for which she is willing to kill all the warriors of Connacht. Even her sons, my own brothers.

"What am I to do?" she said, when I fell before her, shamed and weeping. "Our warriors are no longer willing to fight the Hound."

My father made a harrumphing sound. A sound that clearly said *Who would wish to fight their monster?* But I knew that he would go no further. He never did with Medb; he allowed her license for everything she wished to do and thus he shamed himself. Not that he could have controlled her with any permission yea or nay. But even with me, even with his own daughter, he did not even try.

She dressed me in one of her seduction gowns—diaphanous, almost transparent. She ringed my eyes with kohl and reddened my cheeks with the juice of berries. She spent hours on my hair, curling and pulling. In truth, it was more care than I had received from my mother in the length of my life. Perhaps I endured it for that reason. If so, I am no better than my father.

But when she stood me before the assembled company, when she twirled me about like a Cymri slave, then I thought that I would die. Oh, how I wanted to die.

They bid well enough.

Warrior after warrior.

She was very proud of that, I could see. Proud that her daughter would fetch a good auction price. They were in their cups, and they had forgotten that the bid included battle one on one with the Hound of Ulster, the monster who could never be defeated.

They bid to die, the warriors of Connacht. Simpletons when it came to breasts and thighs. I did not blame them. I blame her. For this night, from this night, I will loathe her.

Forever.

I waded into the water carefully, placing my feet between the stones that lined the riverbed. Moonlight streamed over me like snow; my cloak spread behind me on the water like a tipped sail. When the water reached almost to my chin, I did as my mother had taught me in childhood.

"Let your head carry you," she admonished as I struggled against the current. "Don't fight the water. Your body is the the curraghs of Ériu; let it skim on the surface of the water." But I, naked and skinny, her mouse-brown, desperate child, had never been able to achieve that floating calm. Daughter of Medb of Connacht, afraid of a little water, clinging and thrashing.

Eventually, exasperated by my flailing arms and frightened mewlings, Medb would abandon me mid-river, wading naked to the shore, shaking her head in disgust as my father hurried forward with her cloak. Sodden and terrified, I would paw my way to the riverbank and collapse weeping in the mud.

I remembered this now in utter calm. The overblown moon beckoned with its wide white path across the water. I leaned back beneath it in the silvery light, let my head lift the weight of my body, just as she had taught me to do.

Then I had been five; now I boasted twenty summers. Then I had been naked and shivering. Now I was swathed in my heaviest woolen gown, in my cloak lined with ermine, in my sandals weighted with gold and silver trim. Then my heart had ached for her love and approval. Now I had no heart. And now I was fearless, as clear and cold as this river in moonlight.

Medb would be proud of me now. I shook my head. Not so. Neither Medb nor my father would even know that I had gone. They would think only that I had ridden off with my new husband. Perhaps they were feeling triumphant delight that their little daughter was now the perfect spy in Ulster.

It would be weeks before they realized that I was gone. Even Rochad Mac Faitheman, he to whom they had sold me, did not know.

Well enough. I had always been the one alone. It was fitting to depart in this way. The clouds shifted, silver white across the disc of moon.

"This is what I will remember," I said aloud to the night gods. "This wind, this moonlight, these scudding clouds. I thank you for the gift of beauty at my dying."

I felt the water begin to tug me down from below and I imagined the Others, waiting beneath the surface to take me in, to bear me on the current out to sea, on to Tir Nan Og. Would Froech be among them there, my lost beloved?

I drew in one last breath of air. My face slid beneath the surface and the water closed above me like ice-cold silk. From beneath the water, I kept my eyes open, fixed on the moon, prepared to draw in the breath of water that would carry me to the deep river bottom.

I felt the horse before I saw it, felt the thud of hooves on the river bottom, the churning when the water grew too deep.

Terror overtook me. I could not let him take me!

I sucked in a mouthful of water, drew it into my lungs.

The horse was above me then, snorting and tossing, a black water dragon. I saw the hand descend from the saddle, saw the leather arm shield. The hand closed around my hair. Darkness came up from the sides of my eyes then, closing me in a tunnel, narrowing my sight. I welcomed it. Just before it enclosed me entirely, I felt a swell of pride.

I had defeated him, had defeated them both. My loathed enemy—Rochad—my husband. And my mother.

Cú Chulainn at the Ford

Nathcranntail stared at the boy on the rock. This? This was the boyo that he was supposed to fear? Why, he was a just a boy—perhaps some fifteen years? Maybe more, but he was small. And somewhat chubby.

Nathcranntail patted his own girth, which was, he knew, a bit beyond what was acceptable for a warrior of Connacht.

But this wee boyo.

He was, perhaps, five feet tall. He looked chubby, as though too much body was squashed down into the rubbery skin. He had a round face and cheeks that still bore their baby fat.

He was seated on a rock in the middle of the river, leaning back against its bulk, his face upturned to the sun. His hair was carrot red, wound in tight uncombed curls that looked impossible to tame. He was smiling.

Nathcranntail realized suddenly that the boy was clean-faced. By the gods! The boy was too young for a moustache! The glory of every warrior of Connacht and this boyo was too young to grow one.

Nathcranntail smiled secretly behind his own drooping moustache. Well, well. So, he would win Finnabair after all.

He had been highest bidder, the first to try his hand for the pale lissome body that he saw beneath the transparent gown.

This would be well for him. He would return a hero. He would avail himself of the beauteous daughter of Medb of Connacht. He would marry her, be part of the royal family. He would be wealthy for the rest of his life. He had only to defeat this plump young man.

The rumor was that men of Connacht had returned wounded from their forays against this boy. Some, they said, had not returned. That was why Medb had auctioned her luscious daughter. To sweeten the pot. To get the warriors of Ulster vying for something other than their death. Medb was desperate to get her brown bull. And now was the most advantageous time for combat. Everyone knew that the men of Ulster would be under their cursing at the start of this war, writhing with the pains of labor. Single combat would start this war. Nathcranntail smiled; Medb surely knew how to weight the odds. He had only to defeat this lazy young man who still had no idea that he was here!

Fair combat required that Nathcranntail warn the boy of his presence. It would be dishonorable by the rules of combat to kill the boy where he sat, but the stakes were high. Nathcranntail would take every advantage he could get.

Silently, he drew his arm back and unleashed his spear.

The boy seemed to pluck it from the air. Slowly, lazily, he raised a plump arm and simply picked the spear out of the wind.

He opened his eyes. He stood.

Nathcranntail saw now that beside him, the boy had braced a spancil hoop inside a little cairn of rocks. On it, words were carved in the ancient druid language of Ogham. For a brief second, Nathcranntail wondered how a boy could know the arcane language of the druids.

Nathcranntail himself could not read the words.

As if the boy sensed this, he pointed his hand toward it.

"Do you challenge me then?" he asked pleasantly.

"What does it say?" Nathcranntail asked.

"He who would defeat Ulster must first defeat me."

Nathcranntail laughed aloud. "You're a confidant boyo now, are ye not?"

The boy tilted his head at him. "My tribe has asked me to defend them," he replied. "What else should it say?"

Nathcranntail shook his bushy head. Boys. They were always so cocksure. So immortal. He changed his tack.

"What gave my presence away?"

"I smelled you. Did you not bathe for battle?" The boy sounded appalled. "Of course, after that, I heard your spear. You did not throw it well. It wobbled the wind."

The boy reached into a cleft in the rock and withdrew his own spear, a vicious looking projectile with a barbed tip. "Shall I show you how it's done?"

Suddenly, he flipped Nathcranntail's own spear point down into a cleft of the rock and leapt to its shaft. Now he towered—towered over rock and river as he stood on one leg, perfectly balanced, the spear not wavering at all. His own spear he slid into the toes of his free foot. He held it before him like an iron tree.

Nathcranntail had the sudden sense that he might have made a bad decision. Besides, something was starting to happen to the boy on the spear. The fat had become muscle, an abdomen of muscle, legs like trees, arms of rounded stone. The boy's face was wavering as well; he looked as though he was struggling mightily to keep his visage in check, biting his lip until it bled.

"Why did you choose this?" he asked Nathcranntail through clenched teeth. "Why would you choose to die this way?"

"Our queen held an auction for her daughter."

Now the boy's face underwent a terrifying transformation. His head twisted around, gazing at all sides of the river. His hair stood up, the tips catching on fire.

"She auctioned her own child?" he roared in a voice like thunder, like the angry sea.

It was the last question Nathcranntail ever heard. He had no time to answer, or to ponder the boy's righteous anger over a stranger, before the barbed fishhooks opened in his chest and flung him toward a death that was, he realized, not the triumph he had envisioned at all.

The Role of Single Combat in the *Tain*

Because the Ulster warriors were laid low with the pangs of labor, it would have been dishonorable for Medb to send more than one warrior at a time to fight Cú Chulainn. Nonetheless, she did exactly that, sending hundreds of men in her first salvo. Cú Chulainn killed them all with his slingshot and then sent Medb a message that he would be happy to shift to single combat so that not all of her warriors would die.

Single combat in Ireland, like wrestling, and later dueling (Alexander Hamilton anyone?), was considered an honorable way to settle a dispute, and to preserve the larger army, but it was also a spectator sport, with both sides cheering on and even betting for their champion. Combatants would wrestle or fight with sticks or spears. If one yielded, that could end the contest without bloodshed, but if a loser refused to yield, that almost always led to his death. Combatants often came to these events dressed in their full finery of braichs and cloaks, sandals and tunics, but all that was removed for the fight.

When full armies of the Celts went into battle, as happens later in the *Tain*, they were resplendent with plaid braichs, plaid cloaks, embroidered tunics, golden arm and neck torques, leather belts that carry daggers, short swords or axes, arm shields or bucklers, and large body shields or bosses. The most accomplished of these warriors thundered into battle in chariots pulled by two horses and managed by expert charioteers, allowing the warrior to fight from within the chariot, from the yoke between the horses, or from the ground.

Cú Chulainn and the Wooing of Emer

Fame rode down the road with Cú Chulainn now. It announced him at every village.

And women followed the fame.

The boy was under no delusions that the women found him wondrous. He was still the short and stubby fellow he had always been. But how they loved the war-spasm.

Still, the sport was good, and at seventeen he was happy to have it.

Even so, he tested every woman, giving her a riddle, watching for her answer. Some just giggled and unpinned their cloak brooches. Others looked at him like he had grown two heads instead of one that spun. He never turned them down. He was ever gentle and kind. And though he would tell no one—no one—he was always disappointed when they could not solve the mystery.

Fathers began to offer him dowries, desiring that their grandsons be sired by the Hound of Ulster. These he refused, saying that he could not marry until he had received a druid sign. This was only polite; the truth was that he would not marry until he met a woman who could equal him at riddles and stories, who could speak to him in a language only they would know.

Wives of the Red Branch began to make him offers. These were the women of his fighting companions, and he resisted almost all, begging their pardon, claiming the honor of the Red Branch, though there was little enough of that among his fellow warriors.

Still, his fellow soldiers began to worry. They became determined to find him a wife somewhere in Ulster. They asked in every rath and crannog and more than once the people mentioned Emer, daughter of Forgall.

"They say she has the six gifts of womanhood," said Laeg, Cú Chulainn's charioteer. Laeg was a whip-thin warrior who loved his horses more than any being, save the Hound, so Cú Chulainn trusted his wisdom.

"And what are those, do they say?"

Laeg chuckled, for they both knew the plans of the fighting men to marry Cú Chulainn off and quickly.

"They say she is wonderful at weaving and embroidery."

"Hmmph," was the only response he received.

"They say she has great wisdom and chastity."

"Chastity?" Cú Chulainn chuckled. "Well, that would be different, surely."

"They say she is beautiful of face and voice."

"All women are beautiful."

"They say she has elegant, wise speech."

Cú Chulainn looked up from sharpening the blade of his dagger.

"Wise speech? I think we should pay this one a visit."

"You're an odd one, boyo. You know that?"

"And this judgement from you, charioteer? But what are her weaknesses, do they say?"

"Not her own, but her father, for he is Forgall the Wily. He dotes on her and is most protective. I think he would prefer a prince or a wealthy *boaire* to a boy who transforms to a monster."

"How many people do you think could say that to me and live?"

"Only the ones who love you well."

Cú Chulainn grinned. "This sounds like a good challenge. Let us meet this woman and judge how wise her speech. Let us see if we can defeat Forgall the Wily."

And Laeg began immediately to hitch the horses to the chariot of the Hound.

In the hour before they reached the fortress of Forgall, Cú Chulainn bathed in a lake, scrubbing his body with a bar of scented *sleic*, scrubbing his wild hair, which dried even wilder than before, though Laeg did not tell him so.

He donned his best braichs in his clan plaid of deep reds and autumn gold. Over those he donned his *leine,* the linen tunic brilliant with two embroidered hounds, twined and braided together. Laeg helped him to don his five-fold cloak of crimson red, pinning it at the shoulder with a golden brooch, chased with the images of running hounds. He donned his best sandals, yet unworn by battle or by wandering.

"Well?" he asked when he was ready.

"Splendid," said Laeg. "She cannot fail to look on you and be stunned." Privately, he wished for a comb for the huge unruly hair, but that was a cause already lost and he stayed silent.

The women of the village ushered him into the presence of Emer, who was teaching a class on the waulking of wool to a room full of young girls. They began to giggle and whisper behind their hands before he ever crossed the threshold.

Emer, busy with the twisted wool, did not look up for a moment. And then she lifted her head.

She was indeed lovely, her thick chestnut braid cascading over her shoulders, her eyes the green of a May meadow.

Emer regarded him briefly, then gave him a polite blessing. "May the gods make smooth the path before you."

He responded in kind. "May you be kept always from any harm."

She nodded in his direction and began to lower her gaze again to the wool.

Cú Chulainn untied his tongue. "I have come to speak with Emer, daughter of Forgall."

"Ah," she said, knowing perfectly well who he was. "And from whence did you come?"

Again, the little girls giggled, whispering to each other. Cú Chulainn produced a riddle, spoke it to her bent head.

"From Intide Emna have I traveled."

Emer's head shot up. *Clever, clever boy,* she thought. *For here is the riddled name of Emain Macha. And by this riddle my students are kept from our conversation.* For the first time, she smiled.

And Cú Chulainn was struck dumb.

Emer liked the riddling. "Where have you slept?" she asked.

Cú Chulainn grinned back at her. "In the house of he who tends the cattle who graze on the Plains of Tethra."

"And did they feed you well?"

"We were fed on the ruins of a chariot."

The smile darted across her face. So. He was hungry. She gestured toward two of the servants who lingered in the doorway. "Prepare for our guest a haunch of boar. Prepare for him honey mead, cabbage, and parsnips, and barley bread with thick golden butter. Give him nothing that will remind him of a horse."

Cú Chulainn laughed aloud. Oh clever, clever girl. She had figured out his riddle.

"And how did you come here?" she asked him, curious to see how he would code his journey.

"By the hills of the sea have I come, by the foam of the horses of Macha, over the gardens of Morrigu, past the Four Corners of the World, over the marrow of the woman, between the gods and their druids from first the garden of Lugh."

And on it went. *So, there it is,* she thought. His ancestry. His war deeds. His prowess. Well, he was entitled to that by all accounts. Yet, tucked into that was the fact that he had crossed the Boann to come to her.

"Most beautiful is the river of the goddess," she acknowledged, to let him know that she had translated all his riddling.

"Most beautiful is the woman who knows her name," he replied.

She nodded once, began to turn back to her wool.

"Give me account of yourself," he said.

"And why of this?" She looked up in surprise.

"For it is first of all the knowledge I would have."

She answered him in riddle. "I am the *teamhair* on the hills. I am the watcher who vanishes. I am an eel in a pool. I am a rush out of reach. I am the way of hospitality. I am the road who cannot be entered. I am guarded always by champions."

Cú Chulainn clapped his hands in delight. So. Wild weather, vanishing light, slippery eel, hard to capture, impossible to reach.

"I should like to speak to your father," he said.

"Forgall is stronger than one hundred men. Forgall sees more than any druid. Forgall speaks better than any poet."

He heard her warning. Her father would not be open to his wooing.

"I swear by the gods in whom my people swear that a third of my strength equals thirty. Before me, men avoid the ford. Before me, men retreat from battle. Foster-son and nephew of Conor Mac Nessa am I."

He bobbed his head, encouraging her to understand his prowess, his lineage, his family ties. She shook her head. 'You are a boy, who boasts of warlike deeds. I too was raised in the ways of queenly women."

"But you are brighter than all of these. For you are gifted with quickness of tongue and mind."

"Have you no wife?"

"None, for none was worthy until these riddles were undone."

She took a long, deep breath and then Cú Chulainn made his first mistake. "I see there a plain that would be, for me, the best of resting places." He stared at her white neck, at the start of her deep bosom.

Now her face flamed. "I was raised in chastity and stateliness. No one comes to this plain who has not yet defeated a hundred at the ford. And when he comes for me, he will do battle with nine strong men and yet from each of those, one most brotherly man must be saved."

Her eyes were fixed on him now.

So, her father would go that far. Would send men to battle him. And three of them would be her own brothers. Those three he must save.

He nodded. "If this is the challenge you set before me, I accept it."

"If it is done well, then the offer you have made me shall be taken, shall be accepted, shall be granted."

She raised her right palm and he raised his in answer. Something like lightning jumped between their palms.

When Forgall returned to his rath, his daughters assailed him with the news that Cú Chulainn himself had come wooing, that no one had understood a word that had passed between the Hound and Emer.

Forgall was none too pleased, but he knew better than to challenge the champion of Ulster, the nephew of the king. Still, why should his daughter be yoked to a war dog? That way lay tragedy. He would prefer her hand be given to a king. Was this not wise, he asked his counselor, and the old druid agreed that it was indeed, that one who was wed to a warrior was standing always on the cliff of sorrow.

But he was not called Wily for no reason. First, he ordered a case of good Gaulish wine. Then, he disguised himself carefully, dressed himself as a traveling poet, waited for the great festival at Emain Macha. When he asked for entrée, he stumbled through his Irish, threw in phrases of the Gaulish tongue, pointed repeatedly to his servants, saying "Wine for the good King Conor, whose fame goes before him in Gaul."

He told stories of Gaulish wars, of Roman invaders. He was welcome by the fire for the stories alone. And he bided his time until the night of the praises. One by one the warriors of Ulster stood to praise each other, to praise their great charioteers, to praise their generous king. Many praised Cú Chulainn for his battle prowess, for his generosity and fair hand, for his humility among the Red Branch, but the boy shied away from claiming credit in the company, staying seated and waving his hand in the face of the praise.

Truly, Forgall thought, he seemed a good young man.

But not for his daughter a man of war.

And the only solution for that was to send him away. To send him somewhere where he would be killed. Where Emer could mourn the loss of her first love and go forward.

And so, he stood in the midst of the company.

"If one from Gaul may make some praise," he cried. "for the fame of this boy is known even to us, even on so far a shore!"

At this the company cheered and raised their cups.

"We of Gaul have heard of the great Warrior School of Scáthach of the Western Isles. What honor it would be for this young man to study there, at the greatest of all warrior schools, with a woman who cannot be defeated by any man alive! What honor this would bring to the people of Ulster."

Conor stood from his throne. "Nephew!" he thundered, "our Gaulish guest speaks well for you. Would you be of mind to go to the Western Isles, to study with this woman warrior?"

"One warning," Forgall called aloud, "for I am told she accepts few men. Only the finest warriors will be allowed. Those she does not want, she kills."

Now Cú Chulainn did stand in the company. "She would not reject me," he roared and Forgall noticed that he seemed taller than he had seemed sitting, that the unruly hair seemed to flicker in the firelight.

All the Red Branch warriors slammed their cups on the table then, beating a rhythm as they chanted "Sky ah, sky ah."

"So it shall be!" Conor called over the company. "Our greatest warrior to the greatest teacher. Who will accompany our Hound to Alba?"

Several warriors rushed to stand beside Cú Chulainn.

Only when he looked at Laeg did the boy realize what had just happened. In the frenzy of his war spasm, in the quantity of mead that he had drunk, in the thrall of his warrior pride, he had agreed to depart before winning the hand of Emer. He hung his head in shame and sorrow. Behind his back, the triumphant Gaulish poet slipped out into the night, delighted with his good results, determined next to contact the king of Leinster to discuss his younger daughter Emer, now suddenly of marriageable age.

Dal Riada

Scotland, in the long-ago days, was called Alba. Its western coast and off islands were visited by and eventually occupied by Northern Irish tribes, who came to be called the Dal Riada. Modern DNA studies show strong matches between clusters of Northern Irish DNA with the DNA from the west of Scotland.

Cú Chulainn and the Warrior Women of Alba

Cú Chulainn would go on to train with the women warriors Aoife and Scáthach on the wild western islands off the west coast of Scotland. Most scholars think that the isle of Skye is named for Scáthach. Left, a photo of the Isle of Mull on the west coast of Scotland. These warrior schools were known throughout Ireland and Scotland; they were the equivalent of boot camp and seal training.

These warrior schools became pivotal in Cú Chulainn's life. To reach them, he had to cross a magical bridge that shifted its shape. He did this with his salmon's leap, thus gaining him entry and fulfilling his vow to find Scáthach or die. Once there, he discovers that Scáthach and her sister Aoife are feuding; he fixes the feud, but in the process manages to father a child on Aoife. That child comes to haunt him later in the *Tain*. Here too, he meets his beloved foster-brother Ferdiad, whom he is later forced to battle and kill through a trick of Medb.

Meanwhile, Forgall tries to force Emer into marriage with the king of Leinster, but she tells the king in no uncertain terms that she has decided on the Hound.

Eventually, he does return to Ireland, and he elopes with Emer, after saving her three brothers and killing all of her father's guards. Forgall, in trying to run away from Cú Chulainn, falls off the battlements and dies.

Cú Chulainn and the Morrigu

We wanted the boy for our own. That was fair; after all we had a hand in his conception. He should have been mine, my war boy.

We told him from the very start, when he was just a stripling boy, when I appeared to him as Macha. We told him he belonged to us. We warned him never to reject us.

Humans and their foolish honor.

We waited.

We know how to bide our time. Time means nothing to the three of us. Time wears upon us, truly. Humans should be grateful to be mortal.

When he had more than twenty years upon him, when he knew the ways of women, we prepared. We garbed ourselves in diadems and golden torques. We wore a fine, embroidered robe. Our hands were creamy white, beringed in gold and silver. We sent our Macha form before him, human hair that swayed in the breeze and an ivory bosom as beautiful as any he had pillowed for his wild curls.

We called ourselves the daughter of Buan, King Eternal. That is true enough, for we are purposed to the darkness, immortal as it is, then so are we. We offered him riches and cattle.

Our Hound, he saw right through us.

He knew us as we were.

And he declined.

We told him we would punish him and so we did. When he was battling in the river, we slid beneath his legs disguised as eel. We threw him from his balance. He did not fear us then. He crushed us beneath his warrior's foot; so strong was he, he broke our rib.

Disguised as wolves, we moved among the herds of cattle, stampeded them against his chariot. But did he fear us? He cast a stone from his slingshot. He put out our eye.

Though we were wounded, we shifted as a heifer at the forward of the herd. We ran against the boy, who broke our leg by the discus of a stone.

We determined to kill him then, for he had ruined our disguises.

Macha sat at the crossroads as a hag, for that disguise was all that was left to us. One eye was blind, one leg was lame, one rib was broken. All of this was true. No human could have wounded us this way; we know that well. But we ourselves had hand in luring Deichtine to Lugh. Our war boy has the power of his father, Lugh Long Spear.

How weary he was as he came down the road; had we a heart it would have twisted just to see him.

Macha made to milk a cow. He stopped before her.

"I am thirsty ancient one. Will you give me to drink?"

And so she did, the milk of cattle, human warm.

When he had drunk his fill, he handed back the cup. "A blessing on you old one," he intoned, "both from gods and men of earth."

Our leg was healed then, though we did not let him know it.

"I am thirsty still," he said, so we filled the cup from which he drank.

"A blessing on you crone," he said, when all the cup was empty. "May you straightaway be sound that gave it."

Our rib was healed then, though we still kept that a secret.

A third time, our boyo asked for milk and so we gave it.

"Good was your help and succor woman," he said when he had drunk his fill. "And so a blessing on you for the third and final time."

Our eye was healed.

We shook ourself into Macha's young and queenly form. "Look what you have done," she said. "For you have healed the Morrigu, we who have been troubling you."

"Ah well," said our war boy. "Had I known it was you, I never would have blessed you."

But he grinned when he said it. And we forgave him. Never have we forgiven a human through all of time.

He is ours, the Hound of Ulster. We will sorrow when he dies.

The Role of Geasa in Irish Myth

One of the most unusual aspects of ancient Ireland was the imposition of a *geis* (taboo) or even multiple prohibitions (*geasa)* upon our heroes. These taboos were often a "devil or the deep blue sea" proposition. Some make sense; for example, the king of Ulster was forbidden to hunt alone for a boar in its den. Commonsensical; boars are extremely dangerous, and the king could be killed.

In the Fenian tale of Dhiarmuid and Grainne, Grainne places the Fenian warrior Dhiarmuid under a *geis* that he cannot refuse her if she asks him to marry her. This puts him in a terrible position because she has been betrothed to Fionn Mac Cumhaill, chief of the Fenian Warriors of Ireland. Yet he must not refuse.

The worst of the *geasa* are those that come in pairs. This is what happens to Cú Chulainn. One of his *geasa* is that he can never refuse food that is offered by a woman. The other is that he cannot eat dog. So, later in the *Tain,* when a woman offers him dog, he is trapped between two *geasa* and the result is doom.

The Death of Cú Chulainn

I knew that they would take my love, my beautiful boy with the wild hair and the riddling tongue. I knew that he would die in war. It is, after all, what he wanted.

I did not know that the vile queen would use dark magic against him.

Cú Chulainn told me once that he had courted a glorious death. Cathbad the druid had been then at the hill of Emain Macha, casting the sticks as druids are wont to do. My love was young, my love was just a boy.

"The young man who on this day takes up his arms will achieve glory throughout all of Eire," Cathbad intoned. "His fame will be told until the end of time." And here he paused and looked at the young men gathered about him. "But his life will be short. His life will be hard."

None of the rest of the boys ran straight to Conor Mac Nessa, pleading to be sworn to the Red Branch. Cú Chulainn did. Of course, he did.

To his credit, Conor Mac Nessa laughed in his face. "Come back when you have a beard," he said.

But Cú Chulainn was smarter than his uncle, sure he was. My brilliant riddling love. "Cathbad the druid has said this," he told Conor.

"Said that you should be a warrior?"

"Yes, said that my fame will live forever if I take arms on this day. Uncle, I must fill the prophecy. I must!"

It was true enough I suppose, and Conor took it in. He brought forth sword and shield and had Cú Chulainn swear his fealty. They were in the middle of the ritual when Cathbad entered the room, and questioned why Conor would swear in so young a boy, but it was too late.

The die was cast.

All of them were laid down with the labor pains when that foolish woman began her war. Of course, Cú Chulainn had to battle every warrior of Connacht. Even his own foster-brother Ferdiad was tricked into the battle. It nearly killed Cú Chulainn to be forced to lay him low. For months after that battle, he was so wounded in body and mind that he nearly died. Had it not been for his father Lugh, who sent him healing from the world of sidhe, we would have lost him then.

Yet, while he was laid that low, wicked Medb could not adhere to honor. She broke the code of warfare, marched her entire army into Ulster, marched them to the very border of Emain Macha, where she took her cursed bull Donn Cúailgne.

It must have been a surprise to her when the Ulsterman shook off their ancient cursing, when they chased her back to Connacht. More surprised still she must have been when the two bulls took against each other, when Finnbennach and Cúailgne fought each other horn to horn and died. I thought it funny at the time.

I wish her death, the queen of Connacht. I wish her death each day that I remain alive.

She was shamed by my Hound. Shamed by the men of Ulster. Shamed by the foolish meeting of the bulls. And so she planned revenge. She sought out my husband's enemies—Lugaid Mac Cú Roí who went to the dark ones, who forged three magical spears. The sons and daughters of Calatin, all of them druids, their father slain by Cú Chulainn's hand. But that was war. If you fight for an evil queen, evil will befall you.

Dark magic was abroad, was whispered, rumored, so I betook myself to Conor Mac Nessa by the dark of night when my husband could not know. To have asked for protection would have sullied his honor, my Hound.

But Conor knew. Right soon he knew.

If their magic could take my husband down, Ulster too would fall. Conor Mac Nessa would lose his kingship. It was only the strength of the Hound of Ulster that gave them all their power.

So Conor called a *feis*.

If my husband was surprised by such a thing—a feast where none had been before, when no great ritual occasion was required, he gave no sign. He seemed delighted, called for finery, called for Laeg to polish the chariot and groom his beloved horses.

I am disloyal for telling Conor, disloyal for not telling the Hound what I have done.

But I care not. Within the fortress walls, he will be guarded unaware. He will be protected from their trickery.

And trickery they brought, soon after we arrived. For, from the hill below the fortress, the sons and daughters of Calatin spun the branches and the leaves. They mimicked all the sounds of war. Trumpets and the thundering of hooves.

They would have called my husband's spirit had he heard. He would mount his chariot, sure, and rode to battle. But Conor kept the *ceili* thundering within the chieftain's lodge. Mighty drinking, roars of laughter, pipes and bodhrans, all of us dancing, so that not one warrior knew.

When the magic wore itself to nothing, when the clamor of the feasting stilled in the small hours of the morning, Conor sought me out.

"We cannot keep this clamor up," he whispered. "A good feast is a good feast perhaps for three fine days. But then the revelers grow too full of mead and noise. They long for silence and a pillow made of down."

"What are we to do?"

"Do you remember the Gleann na mBodhar?"

"Glen of the Deaf? I have never been."

"It is a place where no sound may enter. We will send him there."

"To what purpose? So that he can sit and hear nothing? He will be suspicious of that."

Conor blew a long breath out of his mouth. "Wise woman. We will send a troop of warriors." He snapped his fingers. "The boy warriors. We will say they are to train with Cú Chulainn and a group of Red Branch warriors. The boys will be ecstatic!"

I nodded my head. "That will work," I said.

On the third day, my Hound kissed me before he mounted his chariot. His horse, Liath Macha, pranced with excitement. Laeg too danced around horse and chariot, alight with purpose. Warriors with a mission. War boys.

"Smooth the plain before me," he whispered in my ear, our old code, a promise of love.

"The plain is yours in light and darkness," I whispered back.

I thought that I would see him again. I thought that he would brace his arms above me once again. I would have thought of a better, more clever riddle had I known.

His men tell me that an old hag tried to warn him there beside the ford. He saw her washing the shield of a hero and when he stopped to ask her why, she said, "I wash the armor of Cú Chulainn, for today he will die."

They say the daughters of Calatin disguised themselves as withered hags. Upon their fire, they roasted his *geis*—a dog. The one food he was forbidden, his namesake. And then they bade him eat. And he could not refuse a woman. Trapped between two *geasa*, my Hound would opt for honor. He ate, and then his strength was gone.

His men tell me he died standing, mortally wounded by a magic spear, lashed by his own hand to an upright stone.

For three days, he stood alone, his back against the stone. Every army too frightened to approach him until the raven landed on his shoulder. Morrigu, claiming him in death. Then, at last, they knew that he was gone.

What did they wish me to say? That I take joy because the Hound of Ulster died a hero? That I am proud? He had upon him only twenty-seven years. I had with him only ten. We had no child.

In this life, I will never speak of joy again.

Until I cross the water.

Until I enter *Tir-nan-Og*.

When I see him, he will riddle, "From whence have you come to be at my side?"

And I will say, "Over the ash of *Cruachan Ai*, on the wings of a sorrowing raven come I."

He will know then that he was victorious. That he triumphed over his enemies of this world and the Other.

That his name has lived for ever.

Cú Chulainn. The Hound of Ulster.

Chapter 2

The Fenian Legends and the Hill of Tara

The Fenian Cycle is much different from the Ulster Cycle. Whereas the Ulster Cycle of Tales takes place in Northern Ireland and includes the war between Connacht and Ulster over the Brown Bull, the Fenian Cycle takes place almost three hundred years later and centers around the Hill of Tara in Meath.

At the time of the Fenian tales, Ireland was ruled by an *Ard Rí,* or high king, named Cormac Mac Art. Unlike Conor Mac Nessa, Cormac was not a man who was ruled by whims and appetites. He was, by all accounts, a truly good and just king. The stories say of him that during his reign, no one had to pen their cattle or bar their door, because safety and justice were the laws of the land. At one point in the stories, Cormac loses his eye in a wild accident (see my novel *Daughter of Ireland* for that tale). An Irish king who is not physically perfect cannot rule, so Cormac retired. He accepted Christianity and took to writing down three books on Irish law, Irish history, and the instructions for good kingship.

Cormac's standing army was the Fenian army. We will talk more about them in this section, but it is suffice to say that all the great Fenian tales arise from the activities of this army. The hero of the Fenian tales is Fionn Mac Cumhaill (pronounced Finn Mac Cool) who enters the story in the midst of Cormac's reign. This army was regularly required to protect the coasts of Ireland from the incursions of Lochlanders or Norseman who were already beginning to harry coastal Ireland.

Many of the Fenian stories take place on or around the Hill of Tara, which, in Cormac's time, boasted a *Teach Forradh* or teaching school where warriors could train, as could druids, lawyers and bards. It housed a *Grianán* or sun house for the women of the clans where they could retreat in comfort with their children. It contained Cormac's great hall *Teach Cormac*, which supposedly boasted a giant feasting hall with a floor to ceiling carved bronze wall behind the king's dais. Also on the hill was the Mound of the Hostages, which was a burial cairn in which archeologists have found the cremated remains of hundreds of people and the preserved remains of ancient elite people, including the full burial of what was clearly a highly regarded young man wearing an elaborate torque or necklace and carrying a beautiful dagger.

When you visit the Hill of Tara today, you will need to imagine all of these dwellings because the hill is an empty green sward of moving grass, marked by the dips and swells of ancient ditch fortifications. Still, from that high vantage in the wild wind, it is easy to envision the hero Fionn Mac Cumhaill.

Fionn himself is utterly different from Cú Chulainn. For one thing, he is not euhemerized; he is a man, an extraordinary man, but with no supernatural parentage. He is a stunning leader, a man who fully knows the joys and sorrows of human existence, but who is capable of great love and great generosity. He also works and lives from a code of honor that becomes the prototype for this type of hero and shows up again in the tales that surround King Arthur and his knights, as you will see.

The modern barred gate at the Mound of the Hostages on the Hill of Tara and the author, below, telling stories on the Hill of Tara.

Fionn and the Hurling Match

Boys! They were boys!

In all his life, Demna had never seen another boy—had never seen anyone other than his grandmother and Liath the warrior, the women who had raised him.

And here was a field full of boys playing hurling.

Hurling he knew. From his earliest years, Liath had used the sport to teach him warrior skills and he could hurtle across a field, jumping, twisting, leaping over hurdles, always making his goal.

And some of them were not playing it very well.

At first, he was careful to stay hidden in the trees. His grandmother had warned him often enough, had she not?

"You will see other humans," she had said. "But you must avoid them. All of us could be in danger if they saw you. If they knew who you were."

He knew who he was well enough. He was Demna Mac Cumhaill, son of the great chief of Cumhaill Mac Trenmore of Clan na Bascna. The clan that was hunted by Clan Mac Morna. He had never known his father who had died in the winter of the clan wars. He had been raised alone in the forests of Eire, his family deeming it the only way to keep him safe.

But safe meant lonely.

Safe meant that he had never before seen another child his age.

And now, here, there was a whole field of boys playing at a sport at which he excelled.

On the field, a dark-haired boy made a goal.

From behind the rock where he had been hiding, Demna shouted out.

The boy turned in his direction, met his gaze. He began trotting in Demna's direction.

"Hello fionn one," he said cheerfully when he reached him.

"Fionn one?"

The boy pointed at his hair. "Your hair is nearly white. An odd color for a lad our age."

Demna touched his head. His hair was white? This was something he had never known. Nor had he ever seen his face. He patted his nose now, self-conscious suddenly.

The boy grinned at him. "I'm Caoilte. Can you play hurling? We're a man short."

"I can." Demna found that his heart was hammering.

"Dhiarmuid," the dark-haired boy shouted toward someone on the field. "Find this fionn lad a hurley. We've found our missing player."

Later Demna would think that he should have pretended. He should have stumbled across the field, not scored every goal that came his way. He should never have run like the stags of the forest. If he had just done that, nothing would have changed.

But change it did.

The boys on the other team grew angry. Caoilte had tricked them, they called. Caoilte had sneaked in a serious player, a gifted player.

Once they had made each other angry enough, they decided to tackle Demna. They piled on him, pinning him to the ground, bloodying his nose and elbows. He had never been tackled by a team of boys before. At first, he lay on the ground in complete surprise. What to do?

Then he heard Caoilte and the boys of his team yanking the other team off him.

So he helped.

He simply lifted his great arms and threw the boys to the side, like so many rags. When he had enough space, he rolled to his back and used the massive legs to thrust the boys into the air, to kick them across the field. When at last he was clear, he leapt to his feet.

"Great fun," he said to Caoilte. "Thank you."

Caoilte laughed aloud. "Come play again. You would be welcome on our team."

But Demna was already loping toward the edge of the field, heading for the forest.

Caoilte called behind him, "Great game Fionn."

Demna waved with the back of his hand and vanished like a deer.

He loped home toward his grandmother and Liath. How would he tell them this story? He could almost feel their fury already.

The boys on the other hand, retreated to the lodge of Cormac Mac Art, high king of Ireland.

"Well, did you win?" the King asked Caoilte, seeing the boy's victorious grin.

"We won, *Ard Rí*," Caoilte said. "There was a boy who joined us. A fionn fellow that we've never seen before, tall as an oak, with legs like the trunk of a tree. He led us to victory."

"Who was he?" Cormac asked, curious that he did not know so great a champion.

"We don't know. He never gave us his name. He appeared from the forest and vanished back into the forest. But I hope he joins us again."

Behind the good king, Goll Mac Morna, the one-eyed chief of the Fenian warriors of Ireland, scanned the room for other members of his clan.

He had listened carefully to the story of the boy's troop, and he had a strong intuition that he knew the true identity of the forest boy.

He was the son of Cumhaill Mac Trenmore, the former chief of Clan na Bascna. The man who had held the post that he now held.

So this was the boy they had been seeking for fifteen years.

The boy they would need to kill.

The Ancient Sport of Hurling

Hurling may be one of the oldest sports in the world, having been played for three thousand years!

Called the fastest game on grass, hurling is played on a pitch about 150 yards long and one hundred yards wide. At either end of the pitch is a goalpost. In Ireland, fifteen players and a goalie are on the field for each team and their equipment is a hurley (a wooden stick with a curved base) and a *sliotar* (a small, hard ball). The object is to hit the *sliotar* between the goalposts. If the *sliotar* goes over the crossbar, the team earns one point, if it goes under, they earn three points.

Running, tackling, hitting, and passing happen at a breathtaking pace in this ancient game, and until 2010 there was no protective equipment. A helmet and facemask are now required, but the game is still played in shorts, knee socks, and team jerseys.

Women's hurling is called camogie. It is played in two thirty-minute halves, while men's hurling is two thirty-five-minute halves. Camogie also uses a slightly smaller *sliotar*, but it is also wildly popular. Estimates are that more than one hundred thousand Irish and American girls play camogie.

When school is opening and closing in Ireland, you will see all the children in their uniforms and all of them carrying their hurleys, but the game is gaining popularity here in the States, where there are now more than 160 hurling clubs.

Fionn and Finegas

Of course, I knew he would come to me. I knew all right.

For one thing, I knew his grandmother, Bodhmall. years ago and longer, when he was just a wee boy, she had told me that the time would come when the boy would have to escape the ones who hunt him, when he would come to me for tutelage. She was, like me, a druid. We know some things, we people of the oaks.

But that autumn, I knew that the time was coming soon.

What is the use of being a wizard if you don't know things? Though I would consider myself more of a teacher, as much as they will use that word.

Teaching isn't magic . . . except when it is . . . and then they will use the word wizard.

Well, I am old. I will take it now.

On the morning that he came, anyone would have known that he was coming. A deaf wizard could have known. He came like a bog elk, my fionn boy. Crashing through the autumn leaves, banging against the branches of the trees. Snapping and crackling from miles away.

And I was fishing!

Fishing!

The silent art they call it, but not with my fionn boy around.

It was strange, though, that the very moment he appeared around the curve of the river, I caught that salmon. The big one, yes. The one that I had been trying to catch for thirty years. Just at that moment.

I should have known, shouldn't I?

Wizard. Faugh.

I should have known.

He stumbled into the clearing, that golden-white hair alight with sunlight, a look of anticipation on his boyish face.

"Are you Finegas?" he asked me.

Now, who would answer such a thing? I would not, of course. I kept my tongue.

The boy was bleeding, but I ignored that too. It was just a scratch, running from a sickle moon beside his eye. It was wanting to tell me something. I could feel the ancient buzzing in the mound above my thumbs. Something was wanting to tell me something.

But I ignored it.

I had the fire ready. I had the spit set up. Carefully, carefully, I slid the skewer down through the gullet of the salmon. The beautiful salmon. Oh, he was as large as a fire log, the old boy I had been chasing. Speckled like a starlit sky along his back, he was pink and silver on his plump belly.

I knew what he contained, that fish. I knew.

I placed him carefully across my skewer, began to turn him at just the right height above the licking fire.

Soon enough I would know more than I had ever known. Soon enough after all this time.

I turned him and turned him, that salmon. My arm began to tire.

The fionn boy came to stand next to me.

"Grandfather," he said politely. "I can turn him for you."

He must have sensed how important it was to me, because I heard him draw a thinking breath.

"You can go into your cabin and get a little stool. I will turn him carefully and you can return and watch me at my work."

My shoulder was aching by now.

I looked up into his face.

"You are bleeding," I said, because I knew who he was, because I saw in his face all the sweetness and all the hope and all the loneliness of his young life and it twisted my heart.

This is what they don't tell you, those who speak of wizards. We are teachers first. Pupils can be ordinary. Pupils can live below their promise. But some—some live above it. And when that happens, oh how we love them. We come to think of them as ours somehow. Perhaps we live through them.

All of that was waiting on his face.

"Clean yourself," I said, waving my free arm at his cheekbone, angry that I had seen the promise on his face.

He went to the river and put his whole head in the chill water, scrubbing at the cheek.

The boy was tough; I came to learn that right enough.

When he was clean, he threw back the wet golden hair. Light caught in the droplets, arcing through the air like rainbows. Something was trying to tell me something. I stared at the light in that water and I knew.

By the time the boy got back to me, my shoulder was on fire.

I am an old, old man. Days I feel surprised by that knowledge. This day my shoulder knew it right well.

Again the boy offered, "Let me turn it for you, grandfather. I will do it exactly as you want it done."

"Very well," I said. "I will go inside for a stool. But look you now and hear me well. This fish must be cooked perfectly. There must be no blemish on it. Do you hear me?"

"I do. I will take care."

I started for my cottage and turned around. "Do not eat my fish! Do you hear me fionn one?"

"I hear you," he said solemnly, "and I promise. There will be no blemish. And I will not eat the fish."

I hobbled into my dwelling for a little stool and turned to hobble back.

I saw what happened from my cottage door. I saw the blister appear on the underside of the fish. I saw the boy take his promise seriously, press his own thumb down against the blister. I saw him burn his thumb. Burn it so there would be no blister on my fish.

I knew what he would do next.

I hobbled forward as fast as I could, dropping the little stool into the dust.

"No!" I screamed. "No! Do not suck your thumb."

But it was too late. His thumb had already risen to his mouth. Already he had put the burned flesh beneath his teeth.

Thirty years I waited to catch that fish.

The Salmon of Knowledge.

Thirty years.

I watched as the knowledge floored him, knocked him to his knees. Past and present. Good and evil. All the knowledge from the dawn of time. I watched him suck in air, heard him make a gasping noise. I watched as his whole body tumbled into the dirt. By the time I reached him, he had begun to rise, but he knelt before me.

"Wise Finegas," he said. "You will be my teacher. I will strive to learn all things that you teach me. I thank you now for all the years that we will work together. My name is Demna. But all of them will call me Fionn Mac Cumhaill."

Salmon Wisdom in Irish Myth

Many myths speak of an origin tree. Biblically, we hear of the tree of the knowledge of good and evil. In the New Testament, the Christ chooses fishermen as his apostles and tells them that they will become "fishers of men."

Norse myth tells us of Yggdrasil, the tree of life that blooms above the earth and whose roots mirror it below the earth; the tree contains the lives of gods and humans.

In Iroquois (Haudenosaunee) myth, Sky Mother fell through the roots of the tree of life. As she descended, the geese people bore her up and she brought to Earth all of the seeds that she had clutched in her fall.

In Irish myth, the origin tree of the world was a hazel tree, and its nuts contained all knowledge. There was a well beneath that tree in which a great salmon swam. He ate of the hazelnuts that fell into the water, and thus he contained all knowledge. Finegas the Wizard knew this, so each year when the salmon swam upstream, he fished for him, hoping to gain that knowledge, but his apprentice Fionn gained the precious knowledge by accident.

Fionn and Aillen of the Sidhe

Samhain edged toward midnight and the torches cast long shadows on the dewy grass. For a moment, Fionn wondered at the wisdom of torches on this, of all nights. He knew now what he would face there on the edge of the hill. His traveling sword hung in its scabbard down the center of his back, his dagger and short sword in his belt.

He heard a rustling in the small trees behind him and reached for his blade, but the face of his ancient Uncle Crimnall appeared, along with the forest Fenians who had hidden so long from the wrath of Clan Mac Morna. They carried a craneskin bag, stitched with jewels that glittered in the torchlight.

His Uncle Crimnall held it out before him.

"It was your father's sword," he said. "He called the mighty blade *In Cadabolg*."

"Hard lightning," Fionn whispered. He drew the sword from the bag, held it above his head in silence as he regarded the faces of these Fenians who had risked all to bring him here, to set him in this moment.

"Tomorrow, uncles," he vowed to the old men. "Tomorrow we will bring justice to our clan and honor back to Eire."

One by one the men clasped arms with Fionn. Then, silently, they turned and departed down the hill, leaving him alone with the task he must complete.

The wind shifted in the trees at the bottom of the hill, soughing and releasing a spray of late November leaves. He could see the lighted skulls in all the trees that ringed the base of the hill. Samhain was a thin night; a night when the Others could come into the world, some like this Aillen, filled with mischief and malevolence.

Fionn shifted his position, held the sword before him by its hilt;

the blade trembled against the ground. He was afraid; surely every warrior who boasted otherwise was a liar.

It was then that he heard the music—delicate and faraway, it drifted up the side of the hill. Music from a *clarsach,* a small harp. Beautiful and strange. It advanced up the hill, seeming to move of its own accord and then the head of the being appeared just below the crest of the hill.

He was a strange-looking character, this little goblin of a man. His hair was the color of orange fire. He had braided it in some complicated arrangement that looked like twining snakes. His nose was bulbous and looked as though it had been broken. He was, perhaps, four feet tall and his gait was bowlegged and wobbly. His eyes were closed, his head leaning against his harp frame as he fingered the *suantraighe,* the fabled sleeping music of the sidhe.

Fionn himself would have felt that torpor drifting over him, had he not pricked his left hand hard against the point of his dagger. Blood dripped from his finger and the sting of the cut was enlivening.

"So this is how you do it then?"

The goblin's eyes snapped open. He seemed completely surprised to see Fionn there and grinned like a child caught in mischief. His pupils were a flickering yellow and they opened sideways, like the pupils of a goat.

"Ah, they sent a new boy."

"They did."

"They seem overly willing to sacrifice their boy warriors."

"Why do you burn it every year?"

"Well, they put so much effort each year into rebuilding, knowing the futility." He grinned his imp's grin again. "I like that about the human condition. Its futility. Its redundancy. Shall I show you how I burn it down?"

Without waiting for an answer, he pursed his lips and breathed out a thin blue stream of fire.

Fionn felt the hair on his arms singe, saw the fire catch at the corner of his tunic. He slapped at it with his left hand, all the while lifting his sword with his right.

"Fire," the little goblin laughed. "I will burn you and all of this with fire."

"You bring fire," Fionn roared. "I bring Hard Lightning."

In Cadabolg whistled through the air. Fionn crouched down so that he would be at the height of the goblin. The great sword connected with his neck and in two seconds the goblin's head rolled into the dirt.

Fionn lifted it in his singed left hand and stared at the severed head with its look of surprise.

Down the ramp of the Hill of Tara he walked until he found a sturdy sapling. This he hewed down with his blade. He placed the head upon the point of the sapling and climbed back up the long hill. In the soft dirt outside the rath of the high king, he planted the sapling deep into the ground.

By the morning light, he was standing next to the grisly sight, his sword blade resting on the ground, his face alight with anticipation. King Cormac Mac Art came forth into the sunlight.

"So this was our goblin."

"The very one who burned the Hill of Tara year after year."

"You know that some will come against you lad? Especially the men of Clan Mac Morna."

Fionn nodded.

"I do not wish vengeance, great king. My leadership will be always about justice."

The *Ard Rí* nodded. "As is mine, lad. Together we will create an Ireland in which justice is the rule of law and the people do not live in fear. For that, they will remember us forever."

Fionn held the great sword *In Cadabolg* before him, the sunlight casting off the blade.

"By this great blade, I do swear it," he vowed.

The Code of the Fenians

Entry into the Fenian warriors of Ireland required a series of tests that were difficult to pass. A warrior first had to leap into a chest-high pit with only a small buckler or arm shield. Fenians threw spears at him and he had to fend them all off. If he passed that test, he then had to braid his hair and run through the forest while being chased by a *fian*. He could not snap a branch beneath his foot or catch a twig in his hair. The third test required him to recite twelve times twelve poems of the history of Ireland. If he passed all these tests, he had to declare himself *ecland agus dither*, clanless and landless, his family and membership now being the Fianna.

Under Fionn, the Fenians became the standing army of Ireland; he whipped them into shape with a code of behavior that got rid of all previous cattle-raiding and tribal warfare.

They lived in the forests of Ireland during the summer. Ireland was densely forested at the time, and they were required to leave a campsite invisible. In winter, they billeted on the villages of Ireland and Fionn required that they provide each village with meat and wood.

Women were to be treated with respect, there was to be no taking of booty in a war and if a Fenian was responsible for killing the parents of a child in battle, he was then also responsible for finding fosterage for that child. While there were not many women among the Fenians, there were some, and they too had to pass the tests and abide by all the rules.

The sword itself was supposedly forged in the world of the Other; the blade arcing through the air like rainbowed lightning. Originally belonging to the Ulster Cycle, it was later passed to Fionn's clan, to Osian, his son, and eventually, legend has it, to St. Patrick

Just as Fionn's sword *In Cadabolg* is the precursor of Excalibur, Fionn's code of behavior for the Fenian warriors of Ireland is the precursor for the code for King Arthur's Knights of the Round Table.

The Four Festivals of the Irish Year

Samhain: November 30.

This was the most dangerous festival of the ancient Irish world because it began the dark season of the year and opened the doorway to the dark forces of the Other, who would enter the world.

Imbolc: February 1.

This is the feast of the goddess Brigid, celebrating lambs and ewes, fire, poetry, and motherhood.

Beltaine: May 1.

Celebration of Spring, but also a celebration of cattle, who were driven through the smoke of two fires in a purification ritual.

Lughnasadh: August 1.

Named for Lugh, the great hero of the mythic cycle and a celebration of feasting and harvests.

Fionn and the Ghillie Dheacar

Excerpt from *I am of Irelaunde*, c2000 by Juilene Osborne-McKnight. Reprinted by permission of Tor/Forge Books. All rights reserved.

Often warriors from other lands would come to offer their services to Fionn and the Fenians and such a one was the Gilly Dachar. He arrived one day at the Dun of the White Walls on a horse so large that it dwarfed the war horses of the Fenians.

Now the Gilly Dachar himself was a large man, being more than a head taller than great Fionn himself and the Fenians took to calling him the giant and his horse, the giant's horse.

Gilly Dachar was a rough, crude man. He lacked the manners of a Fenian, burping and slurping, eating his meals like a hound, breaking wind in company and laughing aloud.

But his horse was worse by far, for it would not behave in the company of other horses, biting and kicking out, until it broke the leg of a Fenian mount, put out the eye of another and snapped off the ear of a third.

Now among the Fenians was one named Conan Maor. Maor was known for his quick temper and the evil tongue which matched it and when it was his own horse who lost an eye, Conan Maor let loose on the rough Gilly.

"Ye're a bloody brute and no warrior of Eire. We of the Fenians don't wan't ye here," he screamed. "But what makes it worse is that ye can't even handle a horse, a thing a Fenian can do from a boy. That great gallopin beast of yours is a danger and should be shot or tamed and I'm the man to do it!"

With that Conan Maor drew back his spear, but the Gilly whistled and his horse came charging straight for Conan Maor.

Well, there was nothing for it, but to grab the beast by the neck and swing astride. Conan Maor ended up on the back of the huge horse who swung from side to side with such a wild gait that Maor slipped first to the right and then to the left, clinging to the mane of the beast and cursing for all he was worth.

The sight was so funny that Fionn convulsed with laughter as the horse circled the yard, but at last he saw that Conan Maor was weakening and could not hold on much longer. He called to Goll Mac Morna and Dhiarmuid Ui Duibhne to ride flank on the the great horse and stop him, but the horse jumped the gate and took off across the field, with Mac Morna and Ui Duibhne splitting the wind to catch him.

At last they came astride, but the horse would not slow. Both Mac Morna and Ui Duibhne leaped upon the horse's back; now all three of them slipped and slid, pulling each other left and right. Fionn and the Fenians laughed so hard they could barely see them through their tears.

And that was how the Gilly Dachar managed to get astride Fionn's best war horse and ride out across the field.

The minute the huge horse saw the Gilly Dachar coming, he bolted for the east, the Gilly Dachar hard behind him and shouting something that sounded suspiciously like "Go!"

Now Fionn called to the rest of his fian. They saddled horses and rode out after the retreating group. Before them, they could see Maor, Mac Morna and Ui Duibhne bouncing up and down and side to side like children's dolls.

Eventually Fionn came to see that the Gilly Dachar was urging the horse on; the chase went on for two days until at last the whole group came to the sea.

There, Fionn was surprised to see two great warships drawn up in the lea.

The horse of the Gilly Dachar plunged right into the sea and swam hard for the ships, with the now wet Fenian threesome clinging, exhausted, to his back.

The Gilly Dachar would likewise have plunged into the sea, but Fionn's great horse refused. Fionn caught up to them then, and he and his fian surrounded the Gilly Dachar and held him at swordpoint.

The Gilly called aloud to the ships. Boats put out for shore and when they reached the Gilly Dachar, the men made obeisance before him and brought him a fine robe and a golden brooch and a circlet of gold for his head.

Then, in the tones of a cultured man, the Gilly Dachar turned to Fionn.

"You see before you a chief of Britain who has heard of your repute in war. We are harassed on our shore by the Norsemen, and I wished to ask your aid, but first to take your measure.

"I apologize for this trick to bring you to the shore, but if you will accompany us to my country, we will reward you richly for your aid in battle."

By now, Dhiarmuid Ui Duibne and Goll Mac Morna had slid from the back of the Gilly's horse. They were swimming toward shore in their sodden cloaks and braichs, dragging behind them a coughing, sputtering Conan Maor, who could not swim, but who had not forgotten how to curse.

Above the waves, he shouted every curse he remembered, and colored them in with what he would do to the Gilly Dachar when he had him in his hands.

On the shore, Fionn convulsed again in laughter and held out his hand to the Gilly.

"You needed no trick to bring me here," he said, "for my laughter alone would have drawn me. And I will be glad to assist in battle one who has given me this story to tell at the Fenian fires."

The soaking threesome emerged from the sea and Conan Maor crawled up the beach toward the Gilly, his wet cloak dragging, his unceasing curses filling the air.

Though he went with them too, to fight the Norsemen in Britain, Conan Maor's cursing punctuated every telling of the tale for many years to come.

Fionn and the White Deer Woman

Came the day when Fionn and his wolfhounds were hunting in the forests of Ireland when before him on the path, he saw a white deer of the forest. Still she was, awaiting his arrival. Nor did she flee before his dogs, but sat still as Bran and Sceolan licked her cheeks, then lay down by her side.

Fionn knew then, knew full well, of course, that she was magical.

Gently, gently, he lifted her onto his saddle, gently, gently rode back to the fortress at Almhuin, the big dogs trotting at either side of his horse.

He made her a nest of straw and soft grasses there beside his own sleeping pallet and for two nights she curled up there beside him. But on the third night, the moon was full and Fionn awoke.

There, standing beside his bed was the most beautiful woman he had ever seen. Her hair was the color of chestnut leaves, her skin the white of milk. Light streamed down upon her from the smoke hole and for a moment, he wondered if she was real or just a vision from his dreaming.

Until she spoke.

"I am Sabh," she said, "the White Deer Woman. Long ago, the dark one, Donn Dorcha, cursed me into the form you saw before you, but I have watched you in the forests. I have seen your way with the beasts. I know that you speak their tongues, that you too can shift into their shapes."

Fionn rose to his feet. "It is a skill my teacher taught me." Already he was reaching for her slender white hand. Already she was placing it into his huge palm.

And so, they became beloved each to the other. And they had perfect happiness for three years, sun, moon, stars, rain.

And that is more than many of us can say.

Came the day when Fionn and his warriors were called to guard the coasts from the incursions of the Lochlanders.

He drew his closest *fian* to him, led by Caoilte Mac Rónán. "I will ask a difficult thing of you," he said, "for I will ask that you remain behind and guard the White Deer Woman. Watch her always; keep her within the walls of the fortress, for I fear that the Dark Druid will know that we have departed and then he will come for her."

On the hilts of their daggers, his *fian* swore.

In the dark of their chamber, he held Sabh close to him. "Do not leave the fortress," he begged her. "Watch for me from the parapets. I will return to you soon and you will see me from afar."

She promised him that she would do as he asked. She did not tell him the secret she was carrying, not wishing to increase his fear for her.

Sabh was three months bearing with their child.

Day after day she watched for him, sun, moon, stars, rain, walking the high earthen defenses, searching the tree line in every direction. Day by day the child in her belly grew until at last Fionn's whole *fian* could see the waiting child.

"Brothers, we must watch her closely," Mac Rónán warned. "I like it not. She watches for him day and night. We must be always on guard."

Came the day when Sabh was seven months bearing with their child.

From the high parapets, no one heard her gasp, but she saw him, saw him at last. There at the tree line, the white hair, the white horse, the billowing blue and green cloak of her beloved Fionn. Beside him the two great wolfhounds.

At last. At last.

She clambered down from the earthen walkway, ran to the gate of the fortress, ducked through the small door. She was running now, running, her hands beneath her swollen belly, running toward her beloved.

From the parapet, one of the Fenians saw the streaking form hurtling down the long causeway. He looked toward the woods line.

"Brothers," he called, "the chief returns. She runs to him!"

"Follow!" shouted Caoilte Mac Rónán. "Follow hard to heels."

She reached the woods line before them. The *fian* watched as the horseman pushed back the white hood, as the cloak shifted to black, as the huge dogs vanished like smoke.

"No," called Caoilte Mac Rónán. "No!"

The Dark Druid lifted his rowan wand from the arm of his tunic. He touched her once on the crown of her head. All of them saw it, all of them cried out as one, as the pregnant form of Sabh, beloved of Fionn, folded down into the form of a white doe, heavy with child.

Caoilte pelted toward the dark druid, thinking that if he could just save the doe from him, Fionn could bring her home, could reverse the spell in which the dark one had hidden her. But by the time he reached the woods line, both were gone and none of the dogs of Almhuin could pick up either scent.

Three days later Fionn and his bands of warriors returned from defending the coasts, riding jauntily up the causeway of the fortress, calling out to each other, successful in their mission to drive the Lochlanders away.

When they had dismounted, Caoilte stepped before Fionn. He lifted his dagger and tore his tunic. One by one, each of the nine men of the *fian* did the same.

"We offer you our lives O Fionn," said Caoilte, tears streaming down his face, "for we have lost you your beloved."

For a moment Fionn looked confused, but he bit on his thumb.

"Oh you gods," he cried aloud. "He tricked her. The Dark One."

He dropped to his knees in the dirt, his cloak sagging around him. For a moment Caoilte and his *fian* saw him as an old, old man.

Then he stood.

"Will you give me your lives brothers?"

Silently they nodded.

"Then come with me into the forests of Eire and we will search for her. For there is not an inch of Eire that the Fenians do not know, and surely he cannot hide her in all places at all times."

In ten minutes Fionn and his *fian* of nine were saddled and riding toward the woods line where the Dark One had appeared.

Oh there is a sorrow in the telling.

For seven years they searched for her. Ceaselessly. Sun, moon, stars, rain.

And they never found her again.

Came the day when Fionn leaned above a pool of water. Exhausted, ragged, he saw his face in the still pool of water. "Old man," he whispered. "I have gone old in searching for you, love."

He bent low above the water, scooped a cool handful into his palm, and drank deeply.

Behind him, he heard the hoarse and breathy sound of a wolf growling.

He turned slowly.

It was an entire pack, the alpha voicing his displeasure at Fionn's presence.

And there, in the midst of the pack, naked and shaggy, was a boy, a thin, rangy boy of about seven years, his matted hair cascading around his human face. At a signal from the pack's leader, he too growled, his tongue, the tongue of the wolves.

Fionn knew. Oh yes, he knew.

He lifted his thumb to his mouth and bit down. There, in the wisdom of the world, was the tongue of the wolves. Deep in his throat, he gave the pack the news.

The boy was afraid, growling and baring his childish teeth, but Fionn lifted him onto his saddle gently, so gently.

The pack had backed away, watched uneasily from the edge of the clearing, shifting on their paws.

In their own tongue, he reassured them.

Then, he rode home to Almhuin with a wolf boy before him.

He made a nest beside his bed where the boy slept. He fed him gently, raw meat and good milk. He spoke to him always in his own tongue. Calm. No fear. Calm.

Came the day when the boy trotted beside him on all fours into the sunlight of the fortress. At first he was terrified, leaning hard against the leg of Fionn, growling low in his throat. But the way of the wolves is wise, so he watched the men and women of Almhuin and one day, he lifted himself onto his hind legs and began to walk, awkwardly at first but in a few days, he had adopted a loping style that would serve him all of his days.

Winter came and he allowed Fionn to clothe him in warm wools, though Fionn was careful never to wrap him in wolf pelts and no longer allowed the pelts in his sleeping chamber.

Now Fionn began to speak to him in the tongue of Eire, the round vowels and the guttural consonants that shift their shape.

He pointed to objects: *tine*—fire, *capall*—horse, *grian*—sun, *gealach*—moon. Always when he pointed to himself, he said *athair*—father.

Came the day when the boy pointed at Fionn, pushed on his throat, coughed a low sound and sputtered out, "*Athair.*" Then he pointed at himself. And Fionn said, "*Mo mhac.*" My son.

The boy learned rapidly then, his curiosity bottomless, the name for every thing. The way to put the sound of things together.

Came the day when the boy could tell a story.

"My mother was a white deer of the forest," he told the gathered company. "Always she kept her body between mine and the Dark One who came to our clearing. But came the day when we were at opposite sides of the glen and the Dark One came and tapped her with his rowan wand. He made to lead her away, but she turned toward me, her eyes pleading. Something must have moved him, because he allowed her to come to me, allowed her to kiss me here, so that my people could find me."

He pushed back his copper hair and there, at the center of his forehead, was a perfect triangle of white deer skin.

Now Fionn stood before the company.

"Now we will give my son his sacred name, the name that he will carry in the stories for all of time. He will be called Osian. The Little Deer."

The Fenians raised their cups into the firelight and gave a mighty roar.

The boy Osian became the poet and the storyteller of the Fenian warriors of Ireland. His name has lived forever. His tales have been passed from one teller to the next, for the boy Osian learned to move through time. And so, his tales have passed to me. And I have passed them here to you.

As for Fionn, he grew grateful and joyful in the presence of his child, in the memory of Sabh, his mother, and he kept them both in his heart forever.

Sun, moon, stars, rain.

The Meeting of the Old Men

She begged me not to touch my foot on the ground. My beloved one. Niamh Golden Hair.

If she saw me now, she would weep. I hold my hands before my eyes in astonishment. The ancient, withered hands of an old man. When only yesterday I was in the full bloom of my youth, my sinews strong, my thighs controlling the horse that brought me here.

I know now why she begged me not to stand on the ground of Eire, for they have told me here, these who call themselves brothers, that my father has been gone for nigh two hundred years. That there are no Fenians in the land of Eire.

I thought that I was with my love three years. But time does not pass among the Others as it does in this world. Time among the Others is as slow as honey.

They call themselves Christians, these brothers in their homespun brown robes. I do not know what warriors these are, because they carry no weapons. They seem to plow and till. I do not even see them herding cattle.

They have sent me a young man to take down my stories. A scribe he calls himself, a man who writes down the words of tellers. The druids would call for his death, though he seems to think nothing of it.

But he is not their leader. The leader is a boisterous fellow named Patrick, a man who seems so sure of himself and his path, that he does not believe in the world of the Other. He saw me there on the horse—saw me young and strong. And yet he sees this ancient now and does not know that time has shifted, that magic has been done. How can anyone be that foolish? He says that he is Roman. Well, there you have it, I suppose. We knew of them in our day; they had a trading post at Droim Meánach. My father and his Fenians traded there. They were hard traders, the Romans, shouting and gesticulating in every exchange.

The boy is scribbling all of this. I ramble about the Romans like an old man in my cups and the boy scribbles. But I can see that he believes me. He knows where I have been. He knows the tales of Fionn, my father, and of the wolfing boy who sits beside him.

"Is he a good leader?" I ask him. "Your Roman man."

He sets his feathered pen aside.

"He is hard, but fair. He dislikes us. The Irish. He was a slave here when he was upon my years."

I regard the boy.

"Why did he ask you to take the stories?"

"Because the brothers begged him. They cajoled. They said that Fionn was a man of great honor and the stories would do justice to the Christ."

"What clan is the creist?"

The boy's head turned to me and his eyes grew wide.

"The Christ is the son of God."

"Lugh Samildánach?"

He smiled at this. "No. Greater than Lugh. Alpha, says our Padraig, and omega."

I shook my head at him.

"First and last."

"Is he a hard god that your leader is so hard?"

"He is not. Padraig is hard because the Irish enslaved him. He cannot forgive. He must learn to forgive."

"My father forgave one-eyed Goll Mac Morna," I said. The boy nodded and scribbled it down.

I sat then for a long time in silence, while the boy twirled his goosequill and waited. At last, I spoke. "Write this in your book, lad."

He lifted the quill.

"Write that Osian, the poet and the storyteller of the Fenians, was sent to one Padraig, a Roman brother, to tell him stories."

"Who sent you?"

I shook my head. "I know not. But I know that the stories will change his heart. Of this, I am sure."

The boy wrote it down.

"And I know that I must tell them. If I am the last of them, if all of those I loved are gone, I am the only one carrying their stories. I must tell them, before this ancient body crumbles to the dust."

He scribbled away. When his hand stopped, I spoke. This seemed to be the way it worked, this scribbling.

"Because the stories are meant to last forever."

He looked up at me.

"Set that down, lad," I said. I was already thinking of which story I should tell him first. "The stories are meant to last forever."

Legends

Whooo wants to know more?

What Is a Legend?

We tend to confuse or conflate myths and legends, but it's fairly easy to separate the two.

Myths are about the gods. Legends are about heroes. Legends are usually attached to specific geographic locations. Legends often have an actual historical person underlying them. In early Christianity, legends were about the saints.

So, for American purposes, our legendary figures include such real persons as George Washington, Davy Crockett, Sacagawea, Crazy Horse, Sitting Bull, Buffalo Bill, Billy the Kid, Frederick Douglas, Harriet Tubman, Johnny Appleseed, just to name a few. These are real people—warriors, trailblazers, visionaries, outlaws—whose deeds in life were so big that they continued on after death, growing larger, more noble, or more superhuman. Because of our particular geography, many of these tales attach to our American West, a landscape that is as legendary as the people who inhabited it and fought over it, but we have legendary figures from every geography and every period in our history, including now.

Legends are heavily reliant on archetypes, which are patterns of storytelling and of character. Hero legends also often follow Joseph Campbell's pattern of the hero's journey.

Let's look first at archetypes, which form the underpinnings of every human story, novel, movie, play, and you—yes—you:

Archetypes of character are instantly recognizable. We have the **hero or the antihero,** the **sidekick** or the **mentor,** the **wizard** or the **trickster,** the **creator** or **explorer,** the **ruler** or the **everyman,** the **chosen one** or **innocent,** or the **outlaw, the mother, father, caregiver** or **lover.** Note, too, that every archetype can have a light side or a dark or shadow side.

Much of this discussion of archetypes arises from the work of Swiss psychoanalyst Carl Jung, who believed that while we do possess an individual conscious and unconscious human mind, human beings also draw from the deeply inherited river of human experience and symbol. He called this the collective unconscious.

Writers and storytellers play with these archetypes—consciously or unconsciously—all the time. For example:

Harry Potter and Draco Malfoy come to mind immediately as hero and anti-hero. What JK Rowling did so beautifully was to paint both characters with moral strengths and moral failings so that neither was perfect, neither was irredeemable, and both were fully human.

Of course, wizards abound in storytelling: Glinda the Good, Professor Dumbledore, Gandalf the Grey. These archetypes guide us, help us, set us on the right path. A similar Christian archetype is that of the guardian angel.

Humanity tells stories based on these archetypes and this is a game that you can play. Look at the list above and see just how many archetypes you can find in your favorite books and movies. You will discover that there isn't a character who cannot be classified by archetype. You yourself are an archetype of character, that character having been created by your life and your life choices. Jung believed that with counseling and introspection, humans could recognize their dark and light patterns and change or integrate their personalities. In other words, you yourself can change your own archetype. Many coming-of-age or come-to-realize stories allow their characters to do just that.

This brings us to archetypes of storytelling. All human stories have patterns and indeed storytelling seems to be necessary to the human experience (If you want to read a fascinating book on this subject, read Jonathan Gottschall's *The Storytelling Animal: How Stories Make Us Human,* which draws upon neurobiology to argue that stories were a necessary evolutionary pattern to allow human beings to cope with the world).

Archetypes of storytelling include the hero's journey (more on that in a minute) the quest (every *Indiana Jones*), true love's course (think *Romeo and Juliet* for tragedy, *Taming of the Shrew* for comedy), defeat the darkness (*Star Wars* anyone?), voyage of discovery (*Star Trek*—

all of them), and salvation and rebirth (*ET the Extraterrestrial,* among others). While these may be "types" of stories, this certainly does not mean that they are all told the same way, nor do they all end the same way. They are simply a framework that is common to human story.

Most familiar to all of us is the hero's journey, thanks to the work of Joseph Campbell, who codified this form of human storytelling into clear patterns. The hero's journey underlies most of the legends in this section of our book.

In the opening of the story, the hero is living an **ordinary life** (Clark Kent in Smallville, for example or Harry Potter on Privet Drive). Something happens that **calls the character to action,** but s/he **resists that call,** either because s/he is afraid or considers himself/herself unworthy. Sometimes, the hero doesn't want to give up a happy and comfortable life, as with Bilbo and Frodo's life in the Shire. The result is that a wizard or mentor—**a wisdom-keeper**—arrives to convince our hero to action and then the hero crosses the **threshold.**

The second act is full of conflict and characters. The hero discovers **friends and enemies, approaches the danger, undergoes life-changing ordeals, and discovers a reward** (like Excalibur or the ruby slippers, or knowledge that can save the world).

Act three **opens the road home**, but the hero will encounter **one more crisis** from which he must **emerge resurrected**. Now, s/he does **return home**, but **changed** utterly.

Play a little game with the steps of the hero's journey, above. Take *The Wizard of Oz* and apply these acts and steps to that story. Dorothy is our hero. Isn't it amazing to see how perfectly it fits? Evidently something about the patterns of story and character are necessary to our species, because we tell the same patterns throughout all of human history. Yes, we set them in different historical and cultural contexts and yes, we dress them in different clothing, have them speak different languages and eat different foods, but the underlying human patterns of storytelling remain consistent throughout human history. Stories are the living proof that human beings are more alike than different.

The Euhemerized Hero and Transmogrification

Euhemerization: In the world of mythology, this indicates a storytelling which gives supernatural qualities or origins to characters who were probably real people. Both Cú Chulainn and Fionn Mac Cumhaill of Irish legend, for example, may have been actual historical characters who were euhemerized as god/men. Cú Chulainn is supposedly the son of a human female, Deichtine the druidess, and Lugh, the All-Craftsman god of the Tuatha de Danaan. Fionn is of dual human parentage, but he has many supernatural powers, among them "salmon wisdom," which gives him all knowledge of past and present, the ability to understand the languages of animals, and the ability to shapeshift into the forms of animals.

Transmogrification: This literally means to transform in a magical way, but in Celtic mythology it means to shapeshift or disguise, so Fintan, husband of Cesair, transforms as an eagle, Fionn Mac Cumhaill as a deer or a salmon, Cú Chulainn in the *riastradh,* or war spasm, and so on. Morrigu shapeshifts continually in both myth and legend; she is a woman, a wolf, an eel, a heifer, a raven, the wind, a hag and more. Transmogrification is an essential element of all Celtic storytelling.

The Ulster Cycle

Centered in Northern Ireland, in the County of Ulster, this cycle contains the *Táin bó Cúailgne,* (pronounced Toin bo Cooley), the story of the war over the Brown Bull of Cooley. This story pits Connacht against Ulster on the whim of Queen Medb of Connacht who "needs" a magical bull.

The story was written down in the twelfth century, harking back to the ninth and seventh centuries, and taking place in the first century.

The *Tain* itself is bordered by stories called *"remscéla"* or prologue stories, of which Cú Chulainn's conception, his encounter with the blacksmith's dog, and his plunge into the lake are examples. His death story also exists outside the *Tain* but is related to the epic.

The *Tain* is a mirror of its time. Bloody deaths abound. The ancient Irish were quite casual about sexuality. Magic is pervasive in the stories, not just with the presence of Morrigu.

If you would like to read the full *Tain,* two great translations have been done by Thomas Kinsella and Ciaran Carson.

The Fenian Cycle

The Fenian Cycle takes place in the third century and is centered around the Hill of Tara in Co. Meath.

Focused on the Fenian army of Ireland and on their leader, Fionn Mac Cumhaill (pronounced Finn Mac Cool), these stories were also written down in the twelfth century.

The Fenian tales are about an army that lived by a code of honor, led by a fully human hero with war-prowess and druidic powers. It would be proper to say that these tales are more "romantic" than the tales in the *Tain.* Fionn's son Osian and his grandson Oscar play important roles in these tales, as does Cormac Mac Art, the third century high king of Ireland who accepted Christianity.

It is worth noting that an army that lived by a code, as well as Fionn's powerful sword *In Cadabolg,* predate and are reflected in the later Arthurian tales of Cornwall, with their Knights of the Round Table and Arthur's sword Excalibur. These archetypes may be universal, but it is very possible that the stories of the Fenians may have been passed down.

Saints and the Pagan/Christian Shift

Though we don't always think of the saints as legendary, they had to be for Christianization to work at all. The people of Ireland thought of everything in terms of story and everything in terms of human intersection with the non-human world. It is likely that the early saints themselves saw the world in this way; the real and the unreal, the human and the spiritual in constant contact, without the wall that modern western societies have placed between body and soul. Here is a quick look at the Big Five: Brendan, Brigid, Columcille, Kevin, and Patrick and the legends that accrued around them.

The Brendan Boat, created by Tim Severin, duplicates St. Brendan's sailing currach.

St. Brendan is the archetypal journeyer. He was a real person who died around 577 AD, supposedly at the age of ninety-three. He began by founding monasteries. This was a common practice for Irish saints and was eventually responsible for saving education, first in Ireland and even on the Brittany coast of France. (For a superb look at the Irish monastic movement, read Thomas Cahill's *How the Irish Saved Civilization*).

But it was when St. Brendan decided to voyage afar that the legends began to accrue. Someone told him a story of magical lands to the north of Ireland, and he felt compelled to investigate. His ship was not what one would call a seaworthy vessel; it was basically a wicker frame, covered with cowhide and sealed with butter. It was a curragh with a sail. Nonetheless, fourteen intrepid monks chose to join him, and off they went.

For seven years, Brendan and his monks sailed to regions that include the Hebrides, Iceland, and the banks of Newfoundland. In 1976, adventurer Tim Severin, medalist of the Royal Geographic Society, duplicated the journey in a boat that was made of the same materials (above).

The best thing about the legend is the way the story is told in the *Navigatio*, which was written down sometime before 1000 AD. The monks found marble pillars in the sea, a paradisical island of birds that could speak Irish, an island of pure white sheep, an island full of old monks, and even an island full of food and a single resident dog, At one point, they land on what they think is an island, but it turns out to be the back of a gigantic whale called Jasconious.

Theologians say that it is not important whether the journey actually took place or not, seeing it as a metaphor for the journey of the spirit and the obstacles we face on the road (sea-road?) toward salvation.

Given Severin's journey, however, many seafarers say that its probable that Brendan and his monks actually made it to all of those locations, thus being one of the first groups of voyagers to reach North America.

The point in fact is that, after seven years, the monks made it back home to Ireland. As storytellers, we know that cultures tell stories with the cultural and linguistic tools they possess. Imagine that you went out to space in an alien ship; you would try to describe that journey using places and descriptions of things you already knew. How else would monks who encountered all manner of strangeness describe that journey other than to use the points of reference that they knew and frame it as a story? Its weirdness does not negate its plausibility.

St. Brigid. Of all the saints of Ireland, Brigid is the most legendary of all saints. As you will remember from our "Myths" section, Brigid was the most powerful female deity figure of  ancient Ireland. Later, St. Brigid becomes part of the pantheon of early Irish saints.

St. Brigid was supposedly the daughter of an Irish chieftain and a woman who was the slave of a druid. She was born in the mid-fifth century, which would make her a contemporary of St. Patrick in the last ten years of his life. In fact, some of the legends say that it was St. Patrick who converted and baptized Brigid's mother.

Another legend says that she was a source of frustration for her father because she constantly gave away all of his possessions to the poor, even including his chased and jeweled sword, but that the king of Leinster saw her holiness. When she asked for land to build a monastery, a third legend says that the king asked her how much she needed and she replied, "Only as much as my cloak will cover." It just kept spreading out, covering hundreds of acres in Kildare, where she founded her monastery Cill Dara, Church of the Oak.

Brigid was one of the earliest founders of a *conhospitae*, a monastery that had both nuns and monks and ran as a university. There she founded a school that did metalwork and made an illustrated version of the gospels, like the *Book of Kells*. This *Book of Kildare* has been lost to us, perhaps by Vikings

Two of the most fanciful (and least believable) legends say that Brigid put out her eye so that she wouldn't be sold in marriage and that she served as the midwife for Mary at the birth of Jesus.

In the way that myths work, it is very likely that there was indeed a real Christian St. Brigid and that many of the attributes of the pagan goddess were then grafted onto the later Brigid. For example, holy St. Brigid's wells still exist in Ireland and people will take their pleas, photographs, and rosaries to these sites. The ancient goddess was also in charge of fire, and seeing footsteps in the ashes of a fire would mean that she had passed, a custom which endures even in modern times, when people will "smoor" the ashes in their hearth on January 31 so that she may leave evidence of having been there on her feast eve.

The festival of the ancient goddess was called Imbolc and was celebrated on February 1, as is St. Brigid's Day in Ireland. In both pagan times and in modern times, people will hang a St. Brigid's Cross above their door so that she can bless the house.

Interestingly, in 2023, the Irish government named St. Brigid's Day as a national holiday on which businesses will be closed. Parades and light shows, similar to those that occur on St. Patrick's Day are anticipated, and Irish women look upon this designation as a recognition of the feminine in the sacred throughout both pagan and Christian Irish history.

St. Columcille. It is likely that much of the story of Columcille (Dove of the Church, though his name is sometimes Latinized as Columba) is more fact than fiction, but it is such a strange story that it reads like fiction. Colum was born in Donegal in 521, joined the Church at twenty, and founded some thirty monasteries by his mid-thirties. All of that is commendable but not necessarily legendary. Where the story becomes legendary, is when Columcille asks to borrow the psalter (a hand-written copy of the Psalms) from St. Finnian.

Columcille decided that he wanted his own copy of the psalter, copying it line by line in the darkness of the church. Legend has it that light streamed from his fingers so that he would be able to see the copy he was making. However, when he returned the psalter to St. Finnian, Finnian also demanded the copy. Columcille vehemently disagreed, saying that Christian knowledge should be passed on and shared, but the king of Ireland adjudicated the case and ruled "to every cow its calf and to every book its copy." Thus, this became the first copyright case in the history of the world.

Columcille was none too happy. He was a warrior from a warrior family and the dispute started a war in which a number of men died on both sides; some legends say three thousand. Columcille was profoundly guilty over these deaths. Some legends say that he exiled himself from Ireland while others say that he was exiled by the king, but he vowed never to see Ireland again. In fact, many years later when he was asked to attend a meeting and mediate a dispute in

Ireland, he did so blindfolded, so that he would not break his vow.

With a group of twelve monks, he exiled himself to the island of Iona off the west coast of Scotland. There he founded a monastery that was focused on copying books. In fact, the *Book of Kells* was begun in the monastery of Iona and Iona has a reputation as a "thin place," a place in which there have been many spiritual encounters. Columcille is buried on the island. As a sidebar, so is Macbeth as well as his stepson Lulach.

The monastery of Iona off the west coast of Scotland. Not easy to reach, this destination requires a ferry from Oban in Scotland to the Isle of Mull, a drive across Mull, and a second ferry to the island, yet Columcille and his monks came there from Ireland in a hide boat called a curragh.

St. Kevin. St. Kevin (Irish Caoimín) is the founder of the monastic settlement of Glendalough, but legend has it that he was very reluctant to found the monastery because what he most wanted was to be a hermit. Born around 498, Kevin was immediately marked for holiness because his infancy legend says that a cow showed up at his home every day to provide him with milk. His parents were Irish "nobility," so it is probable that they owned more than one cow, but this is a bit of hagiography. After his ordination, Kevin moved into a cave on a hill overlooking the upper lake at Glendalough. This was his goal, and his chief wish was to not be bothered. No such luck.

Kevin's reputation as a deeply holy man spread throughout Ireland and followers simply arrived at Glendalough and began building dwellings in order to remain near Kevin and hear him preach. The monastery grew out of these pilgrimages, and Glendalough is still, today, a holy site of pilgrimage, though also much trampled by tourists.

One of Kevin's legendary attributes is that he was a kind of St. Francis archetype, who communed well with animals. One legend says that a blackbird landed in his hand, built a nest, laid eggs, and hatched her chicks; all the while, Kevin lay absolutely still, never eating or drinking for those weeks lest he disturb her.

The entrance to the Glendalough monastic complex in County Wicklow and St. Kevin's upper lake where he used a cave as his bed.

St. Patrick. St. Patrick is rich in legends. Although he is considered the patron saint of the Irish, he himself is not Irish, having been born in either Wales or Scotland. He gives as his birthplace a location called Bannavem Taburniae; no one has ever been able to find a similarly named village. He was certainly well-to-do, his father being a Roman decurion and his grandfather a Roman Catholic priest, in an era where priests could and did marry. When he was sixteen, he was captured by a slave trader (slavery was common throughout the Celtic world) and he was sold to a sheep owner in County Mayo. Here is where the legends begin.

Patrick himself tells us in his journal (the *Confessio)* that he had not been a religious youth, but in Ireland he was put in charge of sheep and wolfhounds in a stony field in the west of Ireland. His dwelling was a *clochan* (a kind of overturned canoe-shaped stone hut) and that *clochan* became his foxhole. He tells us that he prayed a hundred times a day. He learned to speak some raggedy Irish when he was befriended by people from the local village called Foclut Wood, but mostly he was alone in the elements with his wolfhounds and his prayers.

When he was twenty-two, after six years of slavery, a voice awakened him in the middle of the night. "Look," it said. "I have prepared for you a ship." He was in a stone field on the side of a hill somewhere in County Mayo.

But he arose and began walking, all the way across Ireland to *Baile Átha Cliath,* near what is now Dublin. He went from ship to ship asking the captains to take him home, but none would because he was wearing a slave collar. Then, legend has it, he came to a ship carrying wolfhounds. A wolfhound on its hind legs is seven feet tall and the sailors were terrified of their cargo. But Patrick knew how to tame them. He walked among the massive dogs, made a low sound, and they laid down on the deck and were still. The sailors were only too happy to take him home, but the legend has it that they got lost and ended up in France rather than in Wales. They were starving and the plan became to kill Patrick and serve him up flambé when he said that he would call upon his God. Immediately, a herd of boar appeared.

When Patrick finally arrived home, his parents, who had thought him dead, asked him never to return to Ireland. He agreed. But then, legend has it that the same voice who had offered him the boat awakened him in the middle of the night every night for the next eighteen years. "Boy," it said, "come ye back to Ireland." When he was forty and ordained, he returned.

Legend has it that he founded four hundred churches, converted almost every king of Ireland, and escaped arrest by turning himself and his brothers into a herd of deer. To memorialize this, he composed the *Lorica* (Breastplate) or *Faed Fiada*,(Deer's Cry) one of the most numinous and beautiful prayers in all of Christianity. Below are just two brief excerpts. Tonally, it may well remind you of the poem of *Amergin* in our "Myths" section.

I arise today
Through the strength of heaven;
Light of the sun,
Splendor of fire,
Speed of lightning,
Swiftness of wind,
Depth of the sea,
Stability of earth,
Firmness of rock . . .

I arise today
Through God's strength to pilot me;
God's might to uphold me,
God's wisdom to guide me,
God's eye to look before me,
God's ear to hear me,
God's word to speak for me,
God's hand to guard me,
God's way to lie before me,
God's shield to protect me,
God's hosts to save me

Folktales

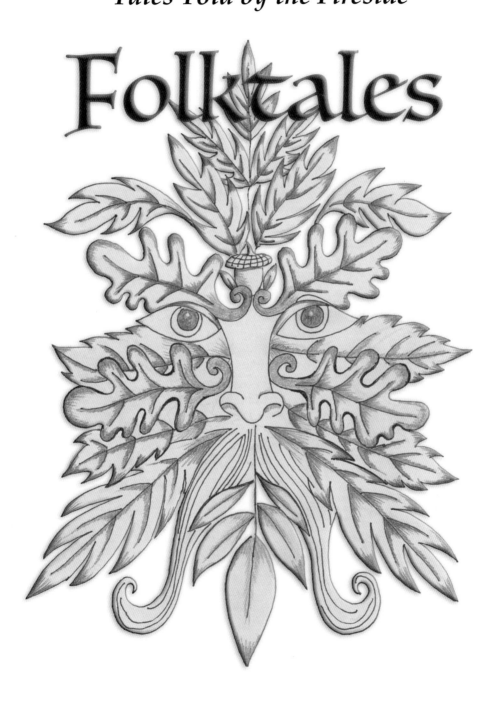

Part III: Folktales: Tales Told by the Fireside

Chapter 1

Giants and Wee Folk

The Canny Leprechaun

(Retelling: Original collected by Jeremiah Curtin as *The Field of Boliauns*)

Daniel O'Rourke planned to be a wealthy man, he did. But you wouldn't call the plan sensible. And no one did.

His plan was to find a leprechaun and steal his pot of gold.

Finding the leprechaun was not that difficult. You waited under a tree, or by the bank of a stream, or behind a hedgerow. Eventually you would hear the sound of humming and the *tap, tap, tap* of a wee hammer.

You have to admire a leprechaun. They work so hard, the little cobblers. They fix unceasing shoes. One shoe at a time. The general theory is that the Fair Folk wear out their shoes with too much dancing and that keeps the leprechauns in work. Your average leprechaun loves to work, he does. This is why he is rich. This is why Daniel O'Rourke formulated his plan.

Daniel had a golden—literally golden—opportunity once when he was a young man. He had found one of the little men tap tapping behind the local pub, but on that day, there had been a bit too much of the whiskey taken, and Daniel had stumbled into the stream and came up dripping, by which time the wee fellow had moved his cobbler's bench and was well and truly gone.

But since that day, Daniel had watched the hanging boughs beside the creek because everyone knows that the little shoemakers are like the foxes and the deer. They follow their tried-and-true paths; they set up their cobbler's bench in their favorite locations. Well, so do we all, do we not?

Daniel had waited years—literally years—when at last the wee fellow set up his bench under the soft green branches of the sighing willow tree.

Oh, he was a natty fellow and Daniel felt proud of himself for waiting for such a splendid shoemaker. His britches were red, his little coat was red, its gold buttons catching the shifting sunlight. His cocked hat was neatly placed and bore a fine feather that liked the breeze.

It was a lucky day for Daniel, sure. No whiskey had been taken and he could stay awake on the far side of the stream while he watched the little fellow. True, the *tap, tap, tap* of the tiny hammer made him long for a nap, but Daniel knew he might not get another chance.

So, he crossed upstream where the water was shallow, came up behind the industrious little fellow, and caught him by the scruff of the neck, holding tight to the collar of his red jacket.

"Ye put the heart in me crosswise," the wee man shouted. "Now what are ye up to Daniel O'Rourke? Do ye not remember the soakin' ye took the last time ye tried this?"

Daniel shook the little man in surprise.

"You knew that I was there?"

"Oh aye, and I knew ye'd take a tumble. I had no worries on that day. And ye did everything just as I thought ye would. Though ye've got me now and I am surprised enough."

"I waited for years," said Daniel, for he was right proud of himself for catching the little fellow. He looked him straight in the eye and he did not break his gaze, though it was hard enough not to blink, but everyone knows that if you look away from a leprechaun, the little fellow will vanish and there will go his gold.

"Gold is what I'm seekin' here," said Daniel, the tone in his voice indicating that he had just thought of the idea. "I'd like to be a wealthy man."

"Would ye now? Well, I am a wealthy . . . man . . . meself, and I have pots of gold buried hither and yon and yon and hither. Put me down and I will take you to one of them, sure enough."

But Daniel O'Rourke knew a lie when he heard one. After all, he told them all the time. So, he shook his head.

"Nay. Do ye take me for a fool? I'll be holding ye right tight here and you will take me to your pot of gold or I will . . ." here Daniel looked around for a good threat, ". . . drown you in the stream. I will so."

The leprechaun nodded sagely. "Well, it seems I have to make a bargain then. So, carry me to the field of gorse, will ye now?"

Daniel marched straight up the hill and headed for the field of golden gorse. Troublesome stuff, the gorse. Once it invades, it takes over. Bushes and hedges and hedges and bushes filled the golden field, but the leprechaun knew the exact burial place of his pot.

"Gold in a golden field, do ye see?" he asked Daniel, and Daniel nodded because it made perfect sense, so it did.

The leprechaun counted—three down one row and three up another—and Daniel saw the wisdom of it because everyone knows that the wee people love when things are done in threes. So, when they reached the bush that was third by third by third, the leprechaun shouted, "Here she is then. One of my finest burial places and I'm right proud of it."

Now Daniel had a true dilemma. He had no shovel, and he couldn't set the leprechaun down to go and find one, for if he did, the wee cobbler would vanish, and Daniel would never again find this precise bush.

He held the leprechaun up before his face and told him what he was thinking.

The leprechaun pondered for a moment and then nodded. "Well, that is a true dilemma, for I must tell you true and truly that if you set me down, I will vanish right before your eyes."

"Don't I know it?" said Daniel, who knew the truth when he heard it. "Now, what am I to do?"

"I have an answer that will save us all."

"Speak then, man," said Daniel, shaking his wee charge by the collar.

"Take off your bandanna," said the leprechaun. "And tie it on the bush."

"I'd have to set you down to do it," Daniel said, shaking his head. "And we both agree that you will vanish."

The leprechaun thought for a long moment and then he lit up in a bright smile. "Why Daniel, I know just what to do. Hand me your bandanna—holding on to me all the while—and I will tie it to the bush."

Danield O'Rourke knew a fine compromise when he heard it. He loosened his red bandanna with his one free hand and gave it to the leprechaun, who tied it to the gorse bush where it fluttered its bright red signal to promise Daniel his coveted gold.

"Well yer honor," said Daniel. "I do thank ye for this fine solution, and now I will let ye go."

He set the little leprechaun on the ground, and where he had been he was no more. Gone. Vanished. Disappeared.

Well, that is the way with leprechauns.

But Daniel was well pleased with his bargain. He ran all the way home and grabbed his shovel from the shed, then ran all the way back to the field of gorse.

Imagine his surprise when he crested the little hill.

For every bush in the field—yes every bush in the field - had been tied with a red bandanna.

Leprechauns and Cluricaunes

As Americans, we tend to think that leprechauns are the ultimate Irish symbol in their green coats and striped leggings. We are wrong on every detail.

Leprechauns are a much later addition to the Irish panoply of Little People. Their name is either a derivation of *leith brogan* (maker of a shoe) or *lugh chromain* (stooping Lugh) which is a diminution of the great hero Lugh Lamhfada of the mythic cycle of stories. Leprechauns are members of a group known as solitary fairies in Irish folklore. They like to sit alone at their cobbler's bench, tapping away, and they take great pride in their shoemaking skills, though they always make just one shoe. They also fulfill the trickster archetype in Irish myth because they are quite rich, hide their gold everywhere, and delight in tricking humans out of that gold. In appearance, they also do not match the American view of leprechauns because their garb consists of a red coat, red breeches, black leggings, cocked hat and buckled shoes.

Cluricaunes are the heavy drinking cousins of the leprechauns. Solitary as well, they live in wine cellars or whiskey distilleries, pubs, or any home that keeps a bar. They can make themselves so small that they fit through a keyhole and once they've attached themselves to a home, they protect its contents from everyone else, although they themselves will "drink you out of house and home," all the while singing and laughing. If you try to move away, they will move right with you, hiding out in your whiskey barrels or beer kegs. How convenient these wee fellows are when your stock of whiskey and wine seems to be diminishing at too rapid a rate!

Finn Mac Cool the Giant

(Likely, this story was originally collected by Patrick Kennedy, but you can find it in dozens of versions)

Giants built the causeway, sure they did. You will know it the minute you step up onto the huge stones. Nowadays, you won't be able to run from Ireland to Scotland the way the giants did in the olden days.

And all because of clever Finn and bad Benandonner.

I'll tell ye the story, shall I?

A long time ago, the giant people used to run between Ireland and Scotland. Well, for the giant people, it was more of a hop, a skip, and a jump.

Best of all was Finn Mac Cool, who loved to sashay back and forth across the water, his great dogs by his side.

How big were the giants of yore, you ask?

Well, picture a tree. Picture the tallest tree ye've ever seen. If you're a Yank, picture a redwood. Go ahead now and picture that tree.

Sure, they were taller than that.

But they got on well, those giants of yore, and they surely loved to visit. Until Benandonner.

Benandonner decided that he wanted to defeat Finn Mac Cool in battle. Mind you, he had never met Finn the giant. But he had heard that Finn was the biggest giant of them all. He had heard that Finn's great dogs were bigger than ponies, bigger than horses, bigger than bog elk, bigger than any four-legged creatures who ever had lived. He had heard that Finn's great stone house was so tall that his towers disappeared into the clouds.

Well now.

Here is the truth of the matter.

Benandonner *was* bigger than Finn. He was twice the size of Finn. His dogs were twice the size of Finn's dogs. His house was so huge that he could look down on the clouds. But he didn't know any of that. So Benandonner was jealous. He thought that if he could just defeat the great Finn, he would be the tallest giant with the biggest house and the biggest dogs.

As it happened, the Little People were returning from a trip to Scotland when they overheard the rumor that Benandonner planned to attack their favorite giant, Finn Mac Cool. So, they went straight to his castle and told Finn's giant wife, who was herself as tall as the tallest tree.

When Finn returned home from leaping across to England and then across the channel, his wife warned him that Benandonner would be on his way.

"Wife," said Finn, "what should we do?" For Finn knew that his own wife was the wisest giantess in all of Ireland.

"I have a plan," she said, "but we'll need to sew you a nightdress and a bonnet. And while I'm doing that, I want you to build a cradle. A great cradle, a huge cradle. But one that is a bit too small for you."

Now Finn grinned at his wife, for he thought he spied the rudiments of a plan, and he liked it very much, he did.

He had barely finished the making of the great cradle when they heard the thundering footsteps of Benandonner crossing the causeway.

Finn slipped into the nightdress and his wife tied the bonnet around his head. Then he crawled into the great cradle. His wife stuck a bottle of milk the size of a bathtub in his hand and then calmly went to answer the pounding at the door.

Benandonner shook his head when he saw her. Why had Finn married such a tiny woman?

"Are ye the wife of Finn?" he thundered.

"I am sir," she said. "But I must say that it is nice to look a giant in the eyes."

"What does that mean?"

"Oh, my Finn is far too tall for me to look him in the eye. He has to pick me up every time we want to have a conversation."

This gave Benandonner pause. But he was distracted by the sound of wailing from within.

"What is that horrible bellowing?" he asked.

"That's our wee babby," she said. "Would you like to see him? He is only a few days old, but he's a beautiful boy."

"And where would your husband be?" Benandonner asked.

"He's leaping," said Finn's wife.

"Leaping where?"

"Oh, he leaps to Europe some days. Other days when he wants a long leap, he leaps away to Afrikay."

Benandonner swallowed hard. He was only able to leap the causeway from Scotland.

"Well, let me see that babby," he said.

Finn's wife led him into the room, where Finn lay in the cradle, his huge feet sticking out the end board of the cradle, his great hand holding the massive bottle of milk. Beside the cradle, Finn's two great wolfhounds lay sleeping.

"Be careful of the puppies," said Finn's wise wife. "They're newborns ye know, but they do love to lay by the babby's cradle."

Benandonner took one look at the massive baby and the huge puppies. Why, he thought, if this is the size of Finn's babies and Finn's puppies, Finn must be twice my size.

Finn's wife watched the face of Benandonner and when she saw what he had concluded she said, "Why here comes my husband now! I can hear him leaping from Afrikay."

Benandonner leapt for the front door then. He leapt for the giant's causeway. He began to leap for home when he realized that Finn the Giant could follow. So, as he hurried back to Scotland, he tore up the great road and threw it into the sea.

Which is just why you can no longer walk to Scotland on the causeway built by giants.

Supposedly the shoe of Finn Mac Cool the Giant, left behind on the Giant's Causeway. A version of this story is told there in cartoon form in the Causeway Visitors Center.

Note the way Fionn, the great leader of the Fianna from our Legends section, is actually diminished by becoming a giant in the folkloric tale here. You will read more about this diminution in our "Folktales: Whooo Wants to Know More" section.

The Giant's Causeway

The Giant's Causeway in County Antrim, Northern Ireland, is a World Heritage Site. The basalt structure was actually formed not by giants, but by volcanic activity and the contraction of cooling lava. The columns adopt an almost pentagonal shape as they march away toward Scotland. Below, the unusual structure called the "organ" at the Causeway.

Dancer Maria Davis, one of Professor McKnight's students, graces the Giant's Causeway.

Chapter 2

Fairy Folk

Wiser than the Wee Folk

(Originally collected by Lady Wilde as *Burn, Burn, Burn)*

They seemed a bit too pale to be human. Or perhaps too small. This was the thought that flitted through the mind of Cathal Mac Murphy as he rode past the house.

He had gone perhaps a hundred yards when the thought came back.

What were the strange twosome doing below the window of the house?

So he tied his horse to a nearby tree and crept back along the hedgerow until he could hear them whispering below the window.

"We will wait until moonlight and place the other one in the empty crib. I have the newborn here."

Cathal peeked through the bushes.

True to her word, the one tiny woman was holding a newborn baby. O'Flanagan's newborn baby with his copper hair. Cathal would know him anywhere. The baby the O'Flanagan's had longed for all these many years.

What to do?

Clearly these were fairy women. If he rushed at them shouting, they would simply vanish like smoke, taking the baby with them.

And then opportunity presented itself.

"Well," said the first little woman in a voice like dried leaves, "leave this one here below the window while we go to collect the changeling. We can't make the exchange until we have the other one in hand."

The first woman nodded and set the baby carefully behind a rosebush below the windowsill. And then, like smoke, they disappeared.

Cathal knew he had only until moonrise, no more. He pushed through the bushes, grabbed the baby, buttoned him tight into his coat, and ran for his horse. He rode home as fast as the wind.

"What have ye done now?" his wife Fionnula berated him when he ran into the house, unbuttoned his coat and handed her a baby. "Ye've stolen O'Flanagan's baby? They'll have your guts for garters, so they will."

"Nay," Cathal whispered. "Hush now. There were women of the Other there. They were going to switch the wee one for a changeling."

Quick as a flash, Cathal's wife Fionnula grabbed a log from beside the fireplace and wrapped it in O'Flanagan's baby blanket.

"Quick now," she said. "Take this back and place it behind the rosebush. In the dark of the moon, they will not know the difference."

And Cathal did as he was told.

In the morning, such a wailing arose from the O'Flanagan household that the whole of the village gathered on the front lawn.

Caitlin O'Flanagan launched from the house holding a bundle in her arms and screaming, "Look what they've done. They've taken my red-haired babby and left me with a changeling." And she held up the baby for all to see.

He was tiny, well enough, but he looked like a wizened old man, his face wrinkled, his hair white, his toothless gummy smile delighted with his new state in life as the pampered child of a wealthy family.

"What will I do?" cried Caitlin O'Flanagan.

Now Cathal stepped forward.

"Why, put him back in his crib of course. The little one will catch a chill. We need to get him warm."

Caitlin tilted her head in Cathal's direction, but before she could launch into further wailing, Fionnula stepped up beside her.

"Do as he says," she whispered, "and all will be well."

So, Caitlin went back into the house, motioning for Cathal and Fionnula to follow. She placed the hideous-looking little man into his crib and made soothing sounds as she tucked his blankets around him.

"Bring him closer to the hearth," said Cathal. "We have to get him warm."

And when the crib was right next to the hearth, Cathal said, "Oh he's just too cold. We need to put some warm coals in his crib."

With that he grabbed a handful of hot coals and threw them in on top of the baby blanket.

With a howl, the ancient creature launched himself up the chimney, scrambling like a spider up and away, vanishing with the smoke.

Now Caitlin sat down at the hearth and put her head in her hands.

"Ye've rid me of the monster," she wept. "But I'll never see my beautiful red-headed babby again."

"Oh, not so," said Fionnula. "For my Cathal has taken care of ye."

Whereupon she led her friend to her own home, where tiny redhead Fingal O'Flanagan looked up in delight at the face of his mama.

And the wee folk, having been defeated by humans, never bothered a single soul in that village again.

The Good People

Fairies in Irish tales are a diminution of the earlier Tuatha de Danaan, who were perhaps five feet tall, lived for thousands of years and were far too preoccupied with matters of gods and war to go about making mischief. But the tiny fairies of folklore spend their time either making mischief or partying all night with music and dancing. Even the ancient *Fir Bolg* diminished in the folklore, becoming pot-bellied fairies who lived in seaside caves. Eventually, in post-pagan folklore, people came to think of the fairies as tiny fallen angels. So as not to offend them, the Irish called the fairies the "good people" or "the gentry." William Butler Yeats said that the fairies of Irish folklore seemed to come in two varieties— solitary fairies and trooping fairies.

Solitary fairies wore red and did lonesome jobs. Leprechauns (shoemakers), cluricaunes (whiskey drinkers), dullahans (headless fairies who drive a death coach), banshees (female fairies who wail over an upcoming death), and changelings (fairies who take the place of human babies) are all solitary fairies.

Changelings must have developed as a way to explain a child who was born with physical, mental, or appearance differences. Clearly, the fairies had stolen the human child and left this changeling in its place. Nonetheless, people cared for the "changeling," because they believed that if they did so, the fair folk would care for their stolen child.

Trooping fairies wear green. They love to dance and play music all night long. Stories say that WB Yeats used to go to the tops of fairy mounds when the moon was full and place his ear upon the ground, hoping to hear their music. Trooping fairies often invite humans to join them and take them on wild supernatural adventures. Trooping fairies live in fairy mounds but meet under and around hawthorn trees. Even in modern times, it is considered dangerous to cut down a hawthorn tree.

A fairy curse or spell was known as a pishogue. If you want to ward off the presence of fairies, you need to carry mistletoe or mountain ash. Fairies are also mightily afraid of iron and fire, so a good fireplace poker beside a roaring fire make strong protection against the fairies.

In Ireland during the nineteenth century, people would often "smoor" the fire before bed, spreading the ashes then making a sign of the cross in the ashes and asking the Trinity to protect the hearth, the home, and the family. This ritual allowed embers to be kindled in the morning but also kept away the fairies. On Imbolc, or St. Brigid's Eve, however, the saint was welcome and people would hope for her footprints in the ashes of the fire, a ritual that carried over from pagan times into Christian times.

The Stolen Bride

(Originally collected by Lady Augusta Gregory)

Ciaran, the king of County Clare, was out hunting by moonlight when he saw four little men carrying a large bier. On the bier was a beautiful sleeping woman dressed in a wedding gown.

The world is full of strangeness, sure, and that we all know.

But this was a bit too strange.

So, Ciaran followed them down the long and twisting road and when they turned toward the base of a fairy hill, he knew that they were up to no good.

Up came his gun to his shoulder and boom—he fired into the night.

He fired over their heads of course. No one with even a smidgen of sense would fire on the fair folk. But the shot startled them mightily and the bier tipped, spilling the white-gowned woman into the snow. Then Ciaran thundered toward them on his great horse. Before his very eyes, he saw a doorway open in the hill and the wee men disappeared.

Well and good, thought Ciaran. Well and good.

He gathered the woman up in the cloth that had covered the bier, draped her over his horse and took her home to his own fortress, where he nursed her back to health, feeding her delicacies from his own table.

She was right beautiful, sure and surely.

She could smile at him shyly.

She could pet his beloved dogs.

But the poor woman could not speak a word.

Ciaran had no idea of her name, or her place of origin, or the story of why the Good People were carrying her on a tablecloth in a wedding dress.

For a year, this went on. Each day her smile toward Ciaran grew warmer and sweeter and each day his heart beat harder when he saw her enter the room, but he did not forget that when he rescued her, the girl had been wearing a wedding dress.

On the anniversary of the night, under a wide full moon, Ciaran went hunting again. He was nearing the fairy mound when he heard laughter and saw the little lights at the top of the hill. Ciaran dismounted and crept along the base of the hill until he could clearly hear their voices.

"He'll have nothing of her surely, for I cursed her tongue the moment we stole her."

"He has the tablecloth?"

"He does, sure enough, but he's human and has no sense of magic. He does not know that if he only fed her from that cloth, her voice would be loosed."

"And how would that serve him, surely? For he would have to return her to her father and that worthy would just wed her to the very one we saved her from."

"Aye. He should have let it go, our Ciaran. She would have been happier here with us."

Now Ciaran was sad as he crept away. A man of honor would restore her voice and send her home. But a man who loved her might keep her forever, silent, but with her beautiful smile.

And to his sorrow, Ciaran knew that he was a man of honor.

That very evening, he spread the tablecloth across his oaken table. His cook made venison and warm, buttered bread, crusted salmon, and tiny honey cakes. For Ciaran, it had the mood of a farewell feast.

The young woman took a bite of the honey cakes and her face lit up.

"Oh my, these are delicious," she said. Then she clapped her hand over her own mouth, her eyes going wide. "Oh my, oh my," she said.

"Who are you?" asked Ciaran, leaning forward with his hand outstretched. She put her tiny hand into his and his heart beat faster. "And how did you come to be with the Good People? And why were you in a wedding dress?"

"I am Clodagh of Kerry," she said, but she suddenly grew agitated.

"Oh, my father. My poor father. For surely, he believes that I have fled."

"Why would you flee?"

"I was to marry the king of County Kerry," she said. "It was a marriage of land and money. I knew that my father needed the wedding, but my own heart did not rest with the king of Kerry."

"Where did it rest?" asked Ciaran, resisting the urge to close his hand around her tiny fingers.

"It did not rest with anyone," she answered. And then she raised her eyes to his. "Then."

"And now?" He thought that his heart might burst from his chest.

"Now it rests with someone."

"Bring the scribe," Ciaran called. "For we must inform Clodagh's father." And he closed his hand around her tiny fingers.

The letter having gone before them, the little party wended its way toward Kerry in the lovely month of May. Around them, flowers bloomed, and birds were singing from the unfurling branches of the trees. Clodagh was gowned in emerald-green finery that Ciaran had ordered for her and each time he glanced at her on the fine white horse he had given her, he gasped with surprise at her beauty.

But all was not well when they reached her father's home. An old man answered the door, an old man thin and sunken in a ragged coat, his eyes faraway and sad. At first, he did not believe that Clodagh was his daughter.

"I sent letters," she protested, but he only answered that he thought they were a cruel hoax.

His kitchen was threadbare, barely enough for tea and no bread or biscuits.

"Why did you abandon me, daughter?" he asked.

Ciaran stepped in then. "She did no such thing," he said. "She was stolen by the Good People, wrapped in your tablecloth, still garbed in her wedding dress. That is how I found her when I stole her away from them."

"Why would they take her?" the old man asked him.

"Perhaps," said Ciaran, "because they knew that she did not love the king of Kerry. For the Good People are a romantic people, as well you know."

Now Clodagh's father hung his head in shame. "Nor he her I fear, for he married another within the month and that woman is already ripe with child."

Now Ciaran did the bravest thing that ever he had done.

"All will be well," he said, "for I do love your daughter, and she loves me. This day we will be married and when we return to my kingdom, you will go with us, and you will never want again."

And so they were. And so it was.

But the next winter, when Clodagh was expecting their first child, Ciaran went hunting once more in the winter starlight. Once more, he saw the little lights atop the fairy mound. Once more, he slipped around the base of the hill, creeping low and quiet.

The Good People were tuning their fiddles, laughing and chatting and then, suddenly, all grew silent.

Ciaran held his breath.

A voice called out into the night air. "Ciaran, King of Clare, we know that ye are there. We did well by ye, did we not, bringing ye a bride? For that was our plan all along. And when your wee child is born, we will dance on the day of her birth, and she will be long blessed."

There was a burst of laughter and a skirl of pipes and fiddles.

Ciaran, the king of Clare, returned home to his wife and his coming child with a full heart of gratitude to the Good People, who are, as we know, romantics one and all.

Shapeshifter Tales

The Merrow Wife

(Originally collected and published by
T. Crofton Croker and Jeremiah Curtin)

Picture a lonely curve of seashore under
a lowering sky. Listen as the breakers roll
like thunder against the wet dark sand.

Picture a solitary man, walking against
the wind, his pipe in his hand. His tobacco
smells like salt and thatch and sea-blown
grass.

Go ahead now. Close your eyes.

Yer man is Michael Malone. He is a
fisherman. Already he knows that the sea
gives, and the sea takes away. He is lonely, our Michael Malone, but
on this day that will change.

For seated on the rocks at the far end of the strand is a merrow.

They are common enough in these parts, the sleek oval bodies and
the dark pleading eyes. Sometimes, when Michael Malone is fishing,
they surface beside his curragh, turning and flipping in the undulant
sea, all whiskers and flippers. Sometimes Michael wonders where
they come from. Is there perhaps a city beneath the sea? Do they
have a language they can speak to each other? Why are their eyes
always watching, always pleading, always so sad? Once, Michael saw

himself reflected back in the eyes of a merrow who appeared beside his curragh. He thought his own eyes were just as sad, though he knew that his were gray.

This day, the little merrow has shifted off her skin and is sunning on the rocks at the far end of the beach. She looks like a human girl. She is far from the little village, and she thinks herself alone, so she has her eyes closed. From time to time, she shifts her human legs from side to side as though she has forgotten that she is no longer wearing her fins. Of course, she is wearing her *cohuleen driuth*, the feathered red cap that all the merrows wear when they are on land. Everyone knows it is the cap that anchors them to the sea. Without it, they cannot return.

Michael knows this.

And she does not hear him approaching over the thunder and growl of the heavy sea.

He snatches the cap, rolls it tight, and shoves it into the sleeve of his fisherman's sweater.

For a moment, she does not react at all, but then the wind shifts her wet, seaweed hair, and she touches her forehead.

In one motion, she sits up, gasps, scuttles back against the stones, and covers her little body with her hands.

Michael regards her calmly. He is a fisherman, and he knows how to still himself and wait. Eventually, he holds out his hand.

She coughs and chokes and makes the sound that someone would make if they had swallowed sea water.

"Man," she sputters. "Will you eat me?"

Michael Malone does not hesitate. "Merrow," he says, for he does not know her name, "I will marry you." He bundles her into his walking coat. She puts her hand in his and he sees that her fingers are webbed. He delights that he will marry a sea woman, that he will not be lonely.

At the rectory, the priest is reluctant to perform a mixed marriage. The girl smells strongly like saltwater and her black hair looks like strands of seaweed. He asks her name, and she makes a sound like water retreating over stones. Of course, he cannot say the sound, so he marries them as Michael and Merrow.

By the firelight, Michael brushes out her hair. It smells like brine, and what fisherman does not love the smell of brine? He tries again and again until he learns to say her name and when at last he gets it right, she lifts her feet and places them together and twirls them in the air. Her eyes are black and the pupils dark, dark brown and round, but Michael fancies in the firelight, that her eyes no longer look sad.

On her first day with him, she walks by the seashore for hours. He will learn that she must do this daily. But on that first day, he uses the time while she is gone to climb into the little loft above the cabin and hide her red cap in the rafters under the thatch. He thinks it likely that a mouse will eat the hat or use it for a nest, but mice are wise to the ways of magic. Always have been wise. So, they ignore the hat, giving it wide berth when they run their evening errands.

The water wife learns to cook and tidy the cabin with a broom. Sometimes she sings in a voice that sounds like rustling autumn leaves, but Michael takes this as a good sign. In due time, there are children—three—a girl and fine twin boys. Michael is proud that all of them are born with webbed fingers because he thinks it shows that both sides of their lineage are in them.

When the girl is ten years old, she goes one day into the loft above the cabin.

"Mama," she calls out, "I have found a wonderful little hat."

She comes down, bearing the *cohuleen driuth* in her hand.

The merrow woman takes the hat in hand. It calls to something in her. It speaks of wind, of spinning in an endless, singing sea. She is unable to resist that call.

She places the hat upon her head.

Her daughter watches as her mother's pupils grow wide and wider.

Then she pulls her little daughter into her arms. "Take care of your brothers," she whispers, "for they will never know what you are about to know." She kisses the little boys' cheeks where they are napping.

"Take care of your da," the merrow woman says, "for now he will be lonely."

The little girl follows her mother to the shore. She watches as her mother's body assumes the shape of water, watches as her mother slides beneath a lighted wave and vanishes into the sea forever.

Picture a man walking alone along a curve of sea. You know him now. He is an old man, our Michael Malone. He is not always lonely, for his sons and daughters have sons and daughters, but he walks here daily, watches the water just beyond the waves.

Sometimes a fine sleek head bobs to the surface out there beyond the breakers. He calls her name then, the word that sounds that water over stones. He wants her to know that her children still love her. He wants her to know that all of them can say her name. He wants her to know that even his little grandchildren have been born with the delicate webs between their fingers and their toes, born of earth and water, wind and brine. He wants her to know that he will love her for as long as the sea sends waves against a shore.

Merrows, Pookahs, and Other Shapeshifters

The idea that animals and humans can shift shape is common throughout all of Celtic myth.

Merrows are called selkies in Scotland, but in Ireland, the word merrow arises from the Irish *moruadh* or sea-maid. In Scots myth, they shed their skin, and the fisherman hides it, but Irish myth gives them the jaunty red cocked hat. The minute they have the hat they return to the sea, no matter the loss, so merrow and selkie stories are almost always sad.

Irish folktales are full of shapeshifters. For example, the story *Brother Wolf* posits a family of lycanthropes, who shift into wolves. Think Professor Lupin in *Harry Potter*. Dozens of Irish stories have characters who shift as swans and geese, as in our *Children of Lir*. The Pookah (púca) whom you will meet in our next story, can shapeshift as a horse, goat, cat, hares, human or any other choice he makes.

Daniel O'Rourke and the Pookah

(Originally collected by T. Crofton Croker)

Sure, you remember Daniel O'Rourke. The very one who thought he had caught himself a leprechaun.

Always in trouble with the Good People was our Daniel.

But on this particular night, he was lucky to make it home a t'all, a t'all. Well, what else should we expect from our Daniel? There was singing at the pub. There was a *ceili*. For Daniel, there was much whiskey taken and it was a long walk home on a moonless night.

Daniel's path to his cottage took him down the single road of the village, past the little church, past the shuttered shops and out to the edge of town, and then onward down the winding road past the ancient Norman keep.

That was where the walk went strange, for Daniel saw lights in the keep and heard the skirling of fiddles and the *thrum, thrum, thrum* of the bodhran. Of course, Daniel needed to explore this, because there might be more singing. There might be more dancing. There might be more whiskey to be had.

And besides, it kept him from going home to his wife who would be none too pleased with him this night.

So, Daniel left the road.

He tried to trudge up the hill toward the keep, but he forgot that many a keep in the long ago day had a moat, or at least a ditch to protect it. That and the much whiskey taken nearly led to disaster, because Daniel lost his footing—or his footing lost him—and he began to tumble heels over head. Just when he thought he would hit rock bottom—or rock bottom would hit him, he heard the thunder of hooves, and a great horse swept up beside him.

"Grab my mane!" the horse commanded, and before Daniel had even a brief moment to wonder why a horse was talking, he was astride the back of the great white beast, and they were sweeping past the keep and up the mountain behind it at such a pace that Daniel thought the horse's hooves were not even firm on the ground. Daniel leaned low and clung to the silky white mane of the horse.

He began to suspect that he was on the back of the Pookah when suddenly the great horse sprouted wings. And then he knew.

But he had no time to contemplate how a horse could sprout wings before the entire beast shifted beneath him and he found himself on the back of a white-tailed eagle with an eight-foot wingspan.

The eagle rose up and up into the sky above the mountaintop and now Daniel was certain he was riding on the back of the Pookah.

"Your honor, sir," he said. "It's getting hard for a human like meself to breathe up here."

"Hold your breath and close your eyes," the eagle replied. "For we are surely going a bit higher."

Daniel did as he was told. He stretched out along the eagle's back and held on tight. He closed his eyes. And in a moment or two, the eagle touched down.

Daniel opened his eyes. The eagle was standing on the surface of the moon. Rocks and stones and no light to be seen anywhere.

"Down you go," the eagle said.

"Your honor, sir," Daniel pleaded. "I don't think I can stay here."

"Well, here now," said the eagle, and he suddenly flew up to where a little hook stuck out from a trapdoor in the side of the moon. "We'll just hang you out to dry for a while."

And he used a massive wing to brush Daniel onto the great hook, where he dangled above the surface of the moon and looked at the blue earth far, far away.

Well, thought Daniel, *this is a fine mess I've gotten into.*

But there was no choice but to hang around, as it were.

After a little while, the door that bore the hook that Daniel was hanging from opened. This was not a sensation that Daniel liked even one bit because he swung wide over open space with his feet dangling, but the little man who opened the door was cheerful enough.

"Well now," he said. "I don't get many visitors, so who would you be?"

"I'm Daniel O'Rourke," said yer man. "The Pookah left me here."

"Ah," said the doorman. "Well, you surely can't stay."

He pressed a lever on his side of the door and shook Daniel loose. Now Daniel was falling, falling toward the faraway earth. It was hard to breathe, and he had no idea where he might land. What if he fell into somewhere that was not Ireland? That would be worse than the moon, surely.

But when he reached the height where he could see the earth below him, suddenly a flock of geese ranged up beneath him, their formation a perfect V.

"Ah hello again, Daniel," cried the lead goose, in between honking to the rest of the flock.

"Yer honor, sir," said Daniel. "Is it ye've returned?"

"Tis," said the goose Pookah. "Tis indeed."

"Well I'm right glad to see ye sir, I don't mind sayin'," Daniel said politely.

"Hold on then, and we'll get you back to Ireland."

And Daniel wrapped his arms around the neck of the goose and clung on until at last in the distance, he saw the lights in the keep of his own village.

"Ye can drop me here sir," he said, and the goose took him literally, tipped him sideways so that Daniel fell through the air, right toward the river at the far edge of his village.

He started to yell to the goose that he might well drown, that he didn't know how to swim, when suddenly he opened his eyes to morning light and to the face of his wife pouring water on his head, where he lay on the ground in the ditch below the keep.

"Here, here now," Daniel coughed and sputtered. "I've had meself a wild night, for I've been ferried about by the Pookah."

"Have ye now?" asked his wife. "And was that before or after you stole O'Malley's horse? Was that before or after you got yourself hooked to the haymow door at Mac Murphy's farm? Was that before or after ye fell in this ditch and got shat upon by an entire flock of geese?"

Daniel regarded her face and thought carefully about his answer.

"Yes?" he said. "Yes, indeed."

Chapter 4

Tales of Wit and Wisdom

The Laziest Girl in All of Ireland

(This story appears in multiple collections as either *The Lazy Girl and Her Aunts* or *The Widow and Her Lazy Daughter.* I tell this story often and my version is below.)

Once upon a time, at a crossroads in Ireland, there lived a widowed mother and her daughter. The daughter was lovely to look at right enough, but she was lazy at the bone.

She never stirred the porridge but she let it burn. She never swept the floor, but the dust rose to the table. She never made her bed or combed her golden hair.

Her mother despaired that nothing good would ever come of the girl.

One day, she had to go to market.

"Girl," she commanded as she donned her coat. "Make your bed and comb your hair. Sweep the floor. Stir the porridge and do not let it burn. I will return and when I do, we will have tea, we two."

Now the dreamy girl had good intentions always. But the dreams got in the way of those intentions. She sat to stir the porridge, still in her nightgown and bare feet, her hair flying every which way. She stirred to the right. She shifted to her other hand. She stirred to the left. But the dream got in the way of the stirring. The girl dreamed that a handsome prince came down the road on a great white horse. She dreamed that he took her to his palace where she never had to work a single day for the rest of her life. While she was dreaming, the porridge burned. She awoke from her reverie to the smell of burning oats and her mother coming back through the door.

Now the mother and daughter were poor enough. They could

not afford to lose even one pot of porridge. So her mother was understandably angry, and she grabbed the broom and chased her daughter into the road.

Barefoot and wild-haired, the girl danced left and right before her mother's swinging broom, laughing all the while.

Meanwhile, a handsome prince came down the road on a great white horse.

Ah, see now where dreaming will get you.

He took one look at the wild scene at the crossroads and he drew two conclusions. The first was that he had never seen anything as beautiful as the barefoot, laughing, wild-haired girl. The second was that Irish mothers should never beat their daughters.

"Woman," he called. "Ye know right well that it breaks the law to beat a child."

Now the mother looked up at the prince on the horse and she drew one conclusion. "Ah your Lordship," she cried, "my daughter never stops working. All the day she works. She sweeps the cottage and stirs the porridge. Why, she has no time to comb her hair or tie her shoes. I just wanted her to have a moment of fun."

And the handsome prince thought how lucky he would be to have a wild-haired wife who loved to laugh and loved to work, so he leaned down from his saddle and put out his arm.

The last sight the widow woman saw was the dirty soles of her daughter's bare feet as the white horse cantered down the road.

But if ye think that's all there is to the story, you are wrong.

For the mother of the handsome prince was also no fool. She took one look at the barefoot girl in her nightgown, with her uncombed hair swirling around her, and she knew. Despite what her foolish son was saying, this was in no way the hardest working girl in all of Ireland.

So, she decided to set her some tasks.

She took the girl to a room filled with straw and sat her before a spinning wheel.

"Now then," she said briskly, "this straw must be woven into good wool. If you can do that by morning, I will see that you have a soft bed and a good rest."

The laziest girl in all of Ireland sat down before that spinning wheel. She waited until the door had closed. And then she did the only thing she could think to do.

She cried.

She cried for a very long time, weeping and snuffling and wiping her eyes with her golden hair. Eventually, the crying made her tired and she leaned her head against the spinning wheel. That was when she heard a knocking at the window of the room.

Over she went to the window and opened it wide. There, below the window frame was a tiny woman dressed all in blue, from her little gown and bonnet to her bright blue shoes.

"Girl," she said. "Why are ye cryin'?"

The girl sniffled. "I'm the laziest girl in all of Ireland," she said, "and I don't know how to spin straw into wool."

For response, the little blue woman sang a song:

Spin and weave
Weave and spin,
Come to your wedding
You'll invite us in.

Then she held up her hand and the girl helped her over the window frame, where she promptly sat down at the wheel and began to spin. The girl did notice that she had a very large right foot, but she said not a word and when the little woman was finished, the room was full of beautiful wool, spun in a glorious array of colors.

"Remember us now," said the little woman as she climbed over the windowsill. The girl wondered how anyone could ever forget what had just happened.

She ran her hands through her hair and stood by the spinning wheel when the queen came through the door. Imagine the shock of that queen when she saw all that soft and glorious wool. She was good to her word and gave the girl a lovely room with a warm bath and a good bed, but when the girl awoke the next morning, the queen was ready with a second task.

Now, at the center of the room was a great loom and the colored wool hung from lines and rafters.

"Well," said the queen, "you did beautiful work with the spinning, so now we need to weave. Blankets and bedclothes and if ye complete it all by morning, I will see to it that you have a fine dress and coiffed hair."

Now the laziest girl in all of Ireland waited until the door closed and she did the only thing she knew how to do. She cried. She had barely launched her wailing when she heard a knock at the window frame. She hurried over and flung the window wide.

Below the sill was a tiny woman garbed all in red from her red gown and bonnet to her buckled red shoes.

"Girl," she said, "why are ye crying?"

"I'm the laziest girl in all of Ireland," she said, "and I don't know how to weave the wool."

Quick as a flash the tiny woman was over the sill and quicker still she worked the giant loom. The girl did notice that she had wide, wide arms, but she didn't say a word. When the little woman was finished, she sang the same song before disappearing over the sill.

Spin and weave
Weave and spin,
Come to your wedding
You'll invite us in

Now the queen was stunned when she saw the lovely blankets and shawls arrayed around the room, but true to her word, she dressed the girl in a lovely gown and a beautiful necklace and had her hair coiffed to perfection. She was taken aback to see that her son, the prince, was even further smitten when he saw the loveliness of the girl, but nothing could be done to change that, so she thought of a third challenge still.

She took the girl to the little room where now only pink and blue wool remained by a pair of knitting needles.

"Booties and bonnets," said the queen. "Fit for a royal grandchild. And if you can complete the task," and here her son the prince chimed in, "we will hold a wedding feast!"

When the door was closed, the girl had barely let out her first wail when she heard the tapping at the window.

She flung open the window and looked down at a tiny woman dressed in a green gown, green bonnet, and bright green shoes.

"Girl," she said, "why are ye cryin'?" though the girl had stopped her crying by now.

"I don't know how to knit," she said.

"I do," said the tiny woman, who seated herself in the only chair and began to click the needles. The girl did notice that she had a very long nose and that occasionally she would hit it with the knitting needles, but she didn't say a word. As the little woman worked, she sang.

Spin and weave
Weave and spin,
Come to your wedding
You'll invite us in.

When the room was full of bonnets and booties in pink and blue, the little woman slipped away, and the queen opened the door to the light of day. The smiling girl was bold now.

"Will ye invite my mother to the wedding?" she asked. "For it was she who taught me to work so hard."

And the queen, who was nobody's fool, was caught in her own trap.

The wedding took place by candlelight, and the great feast had just begun when there was a tapping at the door. The liveried houseman opened the door and saw no one at all, but the laziest girl knew to look down low and small.

And there they were.

"Oh queen," she cried, "my dear aunties have arrived."

And so, the little women in blue and red and green were seated at the dais for the feast.

Now the young prince noticed that the tiny blue woman had a great large foot. "Woman," he said, "where have you come by that lovely foot?"

"Oh, your Lordship," she answered, "this is what becomes of the foot of a woman who must push the pedal to spin the wheel."

"Oh my!" cried the prince. "Then my bride will never spin the wheel again."

Next, he noticed that the little red woman had very wide arms. "Woman," he said, "how is that a woman so small has such wide arms?"

"Ah your Lordship," she said, "this is what becomes of a woman who works the loom."

"Oh no!" cried the prince. "Then my bride will never touch a loom again!"

The little green woman squeezed her very long nose between her finger and her thumb.

"Woman," said the prince, "how came you by that handsome nose?"

"Ah your Lordship," said the woman, "this is what happens when the knitting needles clip the nose again and yet again."

"Hear me!" cried the handsome prince. "My bride will never knit another day."

The three little women went back to their feasting, but the queen raised her glass to her new daughter-in-law who saluted her in kind.

For both of them knew, on that wedding day, that the laziest girl in Ireland had just been allowed to remain that way.

Spin and weave
Weave and spin,
Come to your wedding
You'll invite us in.

The Meaning of a Wisdom Tale

Wit and Wisdom tales are folkloric gems because they tell us that we do not need money or status in order to better our circumstances if we just use our god-given intellect and common sense.

In "The Laziest Girl in Ireland," you will notice elements of "Rumpelstiltskin," but with a much more humorous Irish twist.

In "Honest Jack and His Menagerie," you will be reminded of the "Town Musicians of Bremen."

There are many analogies to "Who Can Defeat the Devil?" but a good American parallel is "The Devil and Daniel Webster."

These wit and wisdom stories exist in every culture's folklore because they offer hope and humor and the sense that the ordinary person can triumph now and again.

Who Can Defeat the Devil?

(Originally collected by Michael Murphy in the 1950s)

Once, long ago in Ireland, there was a poor widower with three children to educate. He pondered this problem for many a day, but there was no solution that he could see. One day when he was sitting in the sunshine by his front door, he saw a strange figure hobbling down the road. As the figure got closer, he heard him singing.

Whack foal de di dee oh
The devil wants your promise
Whack fol de di dee oh
The devil's at the door

And so he was, friends. So he was. He had a fine proposal ready. "Now I see that you are a good and caring father. And I see that you have no money for the education of your dear, young children. So, I'll tell ye what I'll do. I'll educate them all for you. The best schools and the best degrees. And when the last of them is grown and graduated, I'll return, and you'll come with me into the netherworld forever. Now does that seem fair?"

Well of course it didn't seem fair, but it was the only offer that father had and so he signed on the dotted line. Those children grew up and they had the finest educations at the finest schools. His oldest girl opted to be a nun, and the Church sent her for multiple degrees. His second boy opted to be a doctor, and he became renowned for his ability to fix a painful back.

His youngest son became a lawyer.

Well.

When they were all finished with their education, the father told him about the bargain he had made. They felt terrible, all three. Guilty and sad, they sat with their father at the table, by the flickering light of a little candle and they waited for the devil to come to the door and collect his bargain. By and by they heard him coming down the road and he sounded quite cheery.

Whack fol de di dee oh
The devil wants your promise
Whack fol de di dee oh
The devil's at the door

Oh, that cheery song made the daughter mad.

So when the devil rapped on the door, she was ready.

She dropped to her knees. She slapped her palms together. "Lord," she cried, "come and have a look at what this devil has done to a poor widowed man who was only trying to provide for his children."

"Sister," said the devil. "Please stop praying."

Oh, she could clearly see that Old Nick was afraid. She could clearly see that he had had bad traffic with the likes of those she was calling on. So, she prayed harder. "Lord," she howled. "If only the devil would give me Da two more years, I could cease my prayers."

The devil perked up. He always likes to bargain, that one does.

"Sister," he said. "If you'll just stop the praying, I'll give your Da two more years, and he can sign right here."

He produced a contract and her Da signed, well-pleased with his daughter's choice of education.

Now two years went by like this and that. Because they always do.

And once again those three children were gathered at the table in the flickering candlelight, when they heard him coming down the road.

Whack fol de di dee oh
The devil wants your promise
Whack fol de di dee oh
The devil's at the door

But this time, he sounded poorly. This time, he sounded like a man in pain.

"Grab your hat," he said to the father when he came in the door. He was bent almost double, and he was holding the small of his back. "I'm behind on me quotas down there, and I'll be needing your help with the shoveling."

The father stood to take his hat from the rack. A bargain is a bargain after all.

But his son the doctor stepped in. "Nick," he said. "It looks like you are in a world of pain."

"I am," said the devil, clutching at his back.

"Well," said the doctor, "as it happens, I have some skill with the back. If you'll just lay yourself down on this table, I believe I can relieve it."

So, the Devil stretched out on the kitchen table and the doctor pulled one leg forward and one arm backward and when he had the devil tied in knots, he said, "Now if ye'd like me to continue, you'll give me Da two more years."

Well even the devil knows when there is no other option, so they signed the papers and the doc snapped the back and the devil went off down the road in a much more cheery frame of mind.

"We got our money's worth with that boy's education," he was heard to say.

Two years went by like this and that, because they always do.

Once again, the three children were seated at the table by the guttering light of the same small candle when they heard the devil coming down the road.

Whack fol de di dee oh
The devil wants your promise
Whack fol de di dee oh
The devil's at the door

And so he was.

"Why all the sad faces?" he asked when he saw the children. "Ye got four more years out of me, did ye not?"

The lawyer nodded.

"We did," he said, "and you were true to your word. Now, if I could ask for one more thing, it would be for you to give me Da just the time it takes for the stump of this wee candle to burn down to a puddle of wax. Can I ask for you to sit down with us for that long? When there is no more stump, you can have him."

The devil made a disgusted sound. "We wasted our money on this one," he said to the father. "For that's the worst bargain ever. But I'll sit down, sure."

And he pulled out his chair and seated himself at the table.

Together, all of them watched the little candle burn and flicker, flicker and burn.

When there was only a little inch of stub left and when the flame was beginning to sputter out in the wax, the lawyer licked his finger. The lawyer licked his thumb.

Then he pressed them against that sputtering flame.

When a wee stump of candle remained, he picked it up. He put it in his briefcase, and he locked it safely away.

And that father has been living happily with his children since that very day.

Because, as everyone knows, only a lawyer can defeat the very devil.

Honest Jack and His Menagerie

(Originally collected by Joseph Jacobs)

A poor widow and her son Jack lived in a tumbledown shack. The day came when all that remained was enough wheat to make a single bannock of bread.

"Mother," said Jack, "I will go out to find our fortune."

"Jack," said his mother, "shall I give you a half a bannock of bread with my blessing or a whole bannock without?"

"*Muise, maither,*" said Jack. "I would never go into the world without your blessing."

So, he tucked the half loaf into his pack, and off he went down the road. He had not gone far when he saw a poor little donkey sinking into the black peat bog.

"Help me," brayed the donkey, and Jack did not hesitate, for he was carrying his mother's blessing, and he knew that he could help. First, he formed a lasso by twining together the vines that trailed from the trees, and then he threw it over the neck of the donkey. Gently, gently they pulled and swayed and pulled and brayed and at last the little donkey was free.

"I won't forget this kindness," said the donkey. "May I ask where you are going?"

"*Muise,*" said Jack. "My mum and I are poor, and I am off to find our fortune."

"Well," said the donkey, "I may be of help, so I will go with you down the road."

And off they went. They had not gone far when they heard an odd banging sound. Around the corner they came and there was a wee dog with a teakettle tied to his tail.

"Who has done this to you?" Jack asked, offended.

"The bad boys of the village," said the dog, "and I cannot shake it off no matter how I try."

"Here now," said Jack, "I will do it for you."

"I won't forget this kindness," said the dog. "May I ask where you are journeying?"

"*Muise,* I am sent with my mother's blessing to seek our fortune, for we are terrible poor."

"I may be of some help to ye, so I will journey along," said the dog.

"Climb aboard," said the donkey, and the little dog climbed upon the donkey's back.

Again, they had not journeyed far when a little starving cat crossed the road before them.

"Here now," called Jack, "you look terrible hungry." And he broke off some of his bannock and fed the little fellow.

"I will not forget your kindness," said the cat.

"Well, these fine fellows are journeying with me," said Jack. "Now I know you cats are solitary fellows, but you are welcome nonetheless."

"I am with you," said the cat, "and if I can be of help, I will be happy to serve."

And on they went.

A way down the road, a fox crossed their path. In his mouth he was carrying a struggling hen.

From high atop the little donkey, the dog and cat leaped at him through the air. So frightened was the fox that he dropped his hen and ran for the forest.

"Oh sirs," the little hen cackled, "you've saved me from being a fox's supper. May I join you on your wander down the road?"

They made a strange sight surely, the boy walking beside the donkey, the donkey carrying a dog, a cat, and a rooster, who chatted amiably together as they walked the road. Darkness fell and the group made its way into the forest, hoping to shelter beneath a tree, but through the darkness, they saw a little candle in the window of a cabin.

"Look there," said Jack. "Perhaps some friendly house will give us shelter." They all nodded, for everyone knew that hospitality was the law of Ireland.

But oh what they saw when they peered through that window!

For there, feasting at the table were five masked men. And scattered around them was gold and silver, all of it engraved with the crest of Lord Dunlavin.

"Robbers," whispered Jack. "Hiding here with their ill-gotten gains. Friends, what shall we do?"

So, they hid behind the nearby trees and hatched a plan. At least the hen called it "hatching."

Then they crept close to the cabin and Jack counted backwards three, two, one.

"Hee haw!" brayed the donkey,

"Woof woof," called the dog in his deepest voice

"Meow!" screamed the cat.

"Cock-a-doodle-doo!" cried the hen.

Jack looked at her in surprise. "I thought only a rooster could crow," he said.

"Do you see a rooster?" she answered.

And Jack called out, "Level your pistols boys."

By now the robbers were scrambling from their chairs. They burst through the doors of hut and ran into the dark forest. Jack and his companions watched for a while, but they did not return, and they were very hungry. They sneaked into the little cabin and finished the wonderful feast.

"On the morrow," said Jack, "we will return all of this treasure to Lord Dunlavin."

They all agreed that was the best course, and they gathered the treasures into the bags that the robbers had left behind, blew out the candle, and went to sleep.

But once the robbers had regrouped in the woods, they began to have second thoughts.

"It sounded more like a donkey than an army," said one.

"I swear I heard a cat meow," said the second.

"Well, who's afraid of a dog?" said the third.

"Or even worse, a rooster?" laughed the fourth.

Now they all chuckled among themselves.

"Why, what fools we," they said. "For we ran from barnyard animals."

And they crept through the darkness, back to the cabin.

The little dog smelled them coming when they were still a ways away. The little cat hissed and woke the others.

"Friends," said Jack when they were all awake. "Let us 'hatch' another plan."

The robbers entered the pitch-dark cabin. From the lintel above the door, the cat dropped down and scratched the first one down the side of his cheek. He set up a howl.

The second robber pushed in behind him only to be clawed by the little hen who flew and flapped too fast for him to grab her.

The third tumbled in behind only to be bitten once, twice, thrice by the little dog until he had no ankles left to hop on.

The fourth and last never made it through the door for the donkey kicked him into the waiting woods.

"What happened there?" asked the fourth robber when his wounded bleeding companions joined him on the run.

"Clearly," said the lead robber, "we were hit by a woman's carding comb, attacked with the awl and pincers of a cobbler, clawed by the very devil himself, and kicked through the door by the sledgehammer of a blacksmith. That's it boys. They've taken our treasure." And they slunk away to tend their wounds.

Meanwhile, Jack and his companions made their way to the castle of Lord Dunlavin, where Jack asked the porter at the door to see his lordship.

The porter, who was sporting a long, ugly scratch down the side of his face, tried to turn the little group away, but Lord Dunlavin, who was dismounting his horse in the courtyard, heard Jack demanding to see him.

"Here, here," he began, rounding the corner. But then he saw the little menagerie and burst into laughter.

"*Muise,* a blessing on your lordship," said Jack, "for these brave friends and I have come to return your treasure, and I warrant you that the porter of your door is one of those who stole it. Ask him to bring forth his companions and I know that one will have scratches by his eye, one bites across his ankles, and another a purple bruise across his buttocks."

And it was done.

And all of it was true.

So honest Jack was made the steward of the castle and his mother, who had blessed his journey, was given a cottage in the bailey where she lived her days in the lovely company of her son, a little donkey, a wee dog, a fat cat, and a hen who knew how to cock-a-doodle-doo.

Chapter 5

Cinderella Tales

Fair, Brown, and Trembling

Sundays were for husband-hunting, Fair and Brown agreed. They were lovely looking girls, everyone said they were. But they were dim and flickering candles compared to their sister, Trembling.

So they dressed her in rags, and covered her copper hair with a scarf, and left her at home to cook and clean, in company with the henwife who raised the chickens and collected the eggs. After all, they reasoned, a youngest sister should never marry first. (Or possibly ever, they giggled behind their bejeweled hands). And off they went to Mass, dressed in their finest of fine finery.

Eventually the king of Emain Macha took a little shine to Fair, with her golden hair, and began to court her on the church steps.

On that Sunday, the henwife entered the kitchen with a basket full of eggs.

"Ye should be in church, *mo chailin rua*," she said to Trembling. Trembling pulled her duster from the chimney flue and looked at the woman in astonishment. For first things, the henwife never spoke to Trembling. For second things, Trembling was covered in cobwebs and chimney dust.

"None should go to Mass in such a state," Trembling said. She waved the feather duster to emphasize her point, scattering motes of dust in the slant light from the high window.

"Nay," said the henwife. "It's right enough you are. What would ye wear, had ye any wish a t'all?"

"Oh," said Trembling, twirling with her feather duster. "I would wear a gown as white as snow with beautiful green shoes, the color of the hills of Eire."

From the peg by the door, the henwife took down her black cloak with its silver and gold embroidery and swirled it over her shoulders. Trembling wondered, not for the first time, what a henwife was doing with a garment like that. But before she could voice the question, she discovered that she was standing in the kitchen, holding the duster, but dressed in a snow-white gown and emerald shoes. Her scarf was gone, and her copper curls were piled on her head in ringlets. On her right shoulder sat a honey bird, golden in the window light and singing for joy. On her left ring finger sat a honey ring. Outside the door of the house, a milk white mare with a golden saddle and bridle waited patiently for a mount.

"Look ye now," said the henwife. "Don't go into the church. Sit astride this beautiful mare in the sunlight beyond the door and the minute people begin to leave the Mass, you ride away and come straight home. Will ye promise me now?"

Trembling, who was no one's fool, nodded her agreement. She knew right well that magic had been done. But she was wise enough to take the moment's joy.

She followed the henwife's instructions, so she did. The very moment that the church doors opened, and the parishioners started down the steps, Trembling shook the reins of her beautiful mare and galloped away to home.

By the time her sisters arrived at home, Trembling was back at the chimney flue, her tattered dress covered in cobwebs, her copper hair tied up in a scarf.

"Well, me darlins'," asked the henwife, as she always did after every Sunday's Mass. "What is the news from the parish on this lovely morning?"

Fair was clearly quite put out. "Well," she said. "There was a lovely woman on a white horse in a white gown. Her shoes were emerald green, and on her shoulder a golden honey-bird was singing. The king of Emain Macha noticed her, he did. And so, he failed to notice me."

"Well," said the henwife, "how shall we remedy that my fair one?"

"You shall make us matching dresses white as snow," said Brown. "And when we wear them Sunday next, all the princes will forget the white lady on her white mare.

And that was done.

On the next Sunday, when they had departed for Mass, Trembling sought out the henwife in the chicken yard.

"Would ye be wantin' to go to Mass now?" the henwife asked,

grinning up at Trembling, a hen in one hand and two warm eggs in the other.

"Would it be too much to ask?" said Trembling.

"Not a t'all. But help me here to gather eggs and tell me your very dream of a dress."

"Well," said Trembling, for she had clearly been dreaming. "I would love a dress of black satin with red shoes."

The old woman nodded as she put the last two eggs in the basket.

"Shall I fetch your cloak?" asked Trembling, and the henwife laughed. "You are nobody's fool, my girl. Remember that when the time demands."

And in a twinkling, Trembling was dressed in a black satin dress, with a red waist ribbon and red shoes. A bright red bird rested on her shoulder, singing, and the black mare by the door wore a silver saddle and a silver bridle for the occasion.

"Remember your instructions now," the henwife said.

"Stay the saddle and do not enter the church. Ride away like the wind as soon as the Mass is over."

"Nobody's fool," the henwife repeated. "Remember that when time demands."

And off Trembling rode, down the curving road to the church.

This Sunday, all of the parishioners rushed the door at the end of Mass, hoping to see the beautiful woman in the courtyard. Some rushed toward her, and it was all Trembling could do to urge her mare into a full gallop, kicking up dust behind her as she fled down the road.

Still, she was ragged and dirty, lugging coals in a scuttle into the barnyard by the time her sisters' carriage pulled in from Mass.

"Henwife," shouted Brown as she threw herself out the carriage door. "For next Sunday, you will make us both a gown of gleaming black satin with a red sash and red shoes."

Fair was pouting. "The king of Emain Macha tried to chase her down the dusty road. He called to her to return to him. The dress must be exquisite."

The henwife nodded. "But what of mystery?" she said, but neither of the sisters heard her.

When the third Sunday came, the sisters had no sooner left the house in their black satin dresses, but the henwife was pulling her cloak from the peg and swirling it about her head.

"Speak now," she said to Trembling. "What will you wear today?"

When the swirling and the twirling were finished, Trembling stood in the courtyard in a dress with a fitted white bodice and a full red skirt. Over that she wore a green cape and a fashionable hat with three feathers of white and red and green. Her shoes as well were tri-colored with red toes, a white center, and green heels. A green honey bird sang from her shoulder and a red responded from her finger. This time her red hair was left long and flowing, thick with waves and curls. Her mare, returned to her original white color, was nonetheless bedecked with blue and gold diamond spots beneath her gold saddle and bridle.

"Only you could pull this outfit off," the henwife whispered, as her dear girl cantered down the road.

Now, for this Mass, all the princes of Ireland had gathered at the church for they had all heard of the beautiful rider. They were sitting in the back pews closest to the door, each one planning to run for the woman on the horse.

But the king of Emain Macha was himself nobody's fool. He was hiding in the bushes beside the church. Just as Trembling pulled up on her horse, just as the rear doors of the church opened, the king of Emain Macha rushed out from the bushes and ran toward the beautiful girl. The crowd gasped and Trembling cried aloud "Run, oh run," to her mare. But she was one second too late and the king managed to grab a shoe from her left foot before the mare sped down the road.

In the courtyard of the house, Trembling leapt from the horse, distraught, afraid that the henwife would be furious with her.

"I followed all you said," she cried, "but he was hiding in the shrubbery. He stole my shoe."

"Who was he?" asked the henwife, seemingly unfazed.

"I know not," said Trembling, "though he was dressed in ermine cloaks, and his hair was black as a raven's wing for beauty."

"Ah," said the henwife. "Then it's for the best I think. Oh yes, I do."

And she quickly changed Trembling into her rags and scarf and set her to scrubbing the kitchen stairs.

Now all the princes of Ireland decided that they would fight each other for the lady's hand.

"Fools come in every form," the henwife opined when the sisters gave her that news.

But before they could start an all-out war over the mystery woman, lawyers appeared at the door of the king and adjudicated the case, ruling that possession of the shoe constituted the right to search for its wearer.

And so, the search began in earnest—up one side of Ireland and down.—into the tiniest thatched huts and into the mansions of stone. Despite the ruling, all the princes of Ireland searched together, following the king of Emain Macha with the tri-colored shoe. Curiosity is a great journeyer, so.

Some young ladies cut pieces off their toes. Some padded their socks.

None fit the tricolored shoe.

One day, the king of Emain Macha started up the road to the house of Fair, Brown, and Trembling.

Fair opined that he would remember her and that when he saw her once again, the shoe itself would not matter.

Brown opined that her foot was smaller than Fair's, and the shoe would surely fit her.

And then Trembling made her one mistake.

"The shoe might fit me," she said, from behind the handle of a broom.

The two sisters turned on her immediately. They regarded her delicate, but dirty, bare feet. And then they locked her in the pantry closet.

The king of Emain Macha knocked on their door, followed by a retinue of handsome princes. He tried the shoe on each of the sisters, but neither was a match.

Then, from inside the closet, Trembling remembered what the henwife had told her.

"No fool I," she said aloud. "And now is surely the time."

The king of Emain Macha asked, "Are there no other sisters here?"

"No," said Fair and Brown together.

But Trembling called out from the closet, "I am here, and I will fit the shoe."

And so the king ordered the pantry door unlocked.

When Trembling came forth, there was a collective gasp from the princes. Here was a dirty girl, her hair in a scarf, her dress in tatters. But while they were whispering that surely this was not the girl, no one saw the henwife pluck a cloak from the peg by the door. No one saw her disappear into the courtyard.

Then, bit by bit before their eyes, they watched as the girl before them transformed, her copper hair spilling in curls down her back, her raggedy dress transforming into a lovely tricolor until at last, her tiny and still dusty foot, slipped into the little tricolored shoe.

"You will come to my fortress and we will be married," crowed the king of Emain Macha, recognizing the great beauty before him as the girl from the horse.

"Only if my mother can come with me," Trembling said.

"Your mother is dead," cried Fair and Brown, both of them pouting that their sister had outwitted them.

"No," said Trembling. "She is in the courtyard. You will know her, King, for she will be cloaked in silver and gold."

And so, just so, the beautiful dustgirl and the magical henwife moved to the High Hill of Kings.

The Cinderella Archetype

There are more than seven hundred Cinderella stories! Obviously, the theme of the mistreated and underestimated person who rises in the world through magic calls to some deep-seated need in our collective psyche, because people never seem to tire of variations on this story. There are versions in which Cinderella is a man, (remember the Jerry Lewis movie *Cinderfella?*), versions in which birds peck out the eyes of the wicked stepsisters, versions in which gentle Cinderella adopts the wicked stepsisters, brings them to the palace and marries them off, versions in which Cinderella is abandoned by her biological father and survives as a woodland hunter in a tattered coat; the list goes on. Even many recent movies testify to our love of the archetype, from Drew Barrymore's political strong girl Cinderella in *Ever After* to Julia Roberts hooker-with-a-heart-and-humor Cinderella in *Pretty Woman* to Anne Hathaway as the cursed Cinderella in *Ella Enchanted*.

The Ojibwa (Anishnaabe) and the Iroquois (Haudenosaunee) nations tell my favorite version of Cinderella, in which the young sister is badly burned and scarred by fire, her black hair singed and raggedy. The "handsome prince" of the stories is a magical being who draws a sledge bearing sometimes the rainbow, sometimes the Milky Way. To marry him, the girls of the tribe must be able to see him and his magical harness. This adds a component of spirituality to the stories typical of Native Nations values; see well, tell truly. Because no other girls can truly "see" the object of their desire, they make up a "vision." It is the true vision of the Cinderella of the story which wins her true love. Also, in the Native versions of the story, it is often the sister of the hero who plays "fairy godmother," admonishing all the girls to be truthful, rewarding the cinder girl for her true vision not with coaches and horsemen, but with a ritual bath or baptism of complete transformation. This is also in keeping with the matriarchal wisdom archetypes of Native Nations. To hear my Huron/Shoshone friend Eileen Charbonneau, my "sister in story," tell this tale always brings tears to my eyes.

There are two Irish versions of the Cinderella story. In the earlier version, the Cinderella character is a boy, as you will see below in my retelling of "Buachaill Bó Beag." Gaelic historian Douglas Hyde called this story the Brackett Bull, but the Cinderella character is actually a diminutive version of the early Ulster hero Cú Chulainn. He is Buachaill Bó Beag, the little cowboy, (called Billy Beag in many of the stories). He is a short fellow with huge feet, able to cover great distances in a bound. His "fairy godfather" is a bull, who gives the boy his own tail as protection and talisman. He has many adventures, all of which occur in multiples of three, the sacred Celtic number. Eventually, the cattle boy slays a dragon, wins a princess, and leaves behind a giant boot. The stubborn princess will marry no prince, but the cattle boy who owns the boot. Such archetypes are consistent with early Irish life, in which ownership of cattle was the measure of wealth, bulls were indeed magical (remember the great Irish epic the Táin bó Cúailgne from our "Legends" section) and women were strong, stubborn and capable of making their own decisions. Folklorists say that there are more than six hundred versions of this story of a boy who must complete three tasks to win the hand of a princess.

A still later version conflates the cowboy with the story of Trembling. There are dozens of variations on this story. Called "Fair, Brown, and Trembling," it tells of three sisters, two of whom mistreat the third. In an unusual twist, the fairy godmother is a wise woman or druid, a left-over pagan woman of tremendous power, who sends Trembling to Mass in beautiful gowns. In the conflated version of this story, one of the sisters pushes Trembling into the sea, thinking that she will take Trembling's place with the prince, who figures out the subterfuge when his sword remains cold near the pretender. Trembling is swallowed by a sea dragon (a whale in some versions) and rescued by a small cattle boy, who kills the dragon on her behalf. In gratitude, he is brought to live in the palace, raised as the child of Trembling and the prince, where, eventually, he marries their daughter, thus tying together the Irish Cinderella with the Irish Cinderfella.

Buachaill Bó Beag, the Irish Cinderfella

Oh he was an odd one, the Buachaill Bó Beag. He was shorter than all the other boys, and not a bit of handsome. His red hair stood up around his head like a wild forest fire, and he had a lopsided smile and huge ungainly feet, like a clumsy puppy.

Some said he was a boy that only a mother could love, for it was surely true that his mother loved him beyond the beyond.

But he was smart and funny, with a quick wit that made everyone in the tribe laugh. Never mind that he was the son of the king and queen of the tuath; he put on no airs a t'all and all the tribe loved him for that as well.

His best friend was a magical bull that had once belonged to his mother the queen. Bó Beag called the great beast Corcaigh and the two were inseparable, wandering the fields of Ireland, the boy telling stories and singing songs, the bull watching him like a great horned grandfather.

Oh, it made everyone happy to see them together.

And then, as will happen in life, sorrow came calling. The mother of Bó Beag grew very ill, and she knew that she was not long for this world. She called her husband to her.

"Hear me now, King of Corc," she whispered. "You must never part Corcaigh and Buachaill Bó Beag, for each protects the other. When I am gone, my boy will need his bull to hold his happiness."

And the king promised solemnly, with tears in his eyes.

But not long after the queen had died, the king grew lonely for a new companion. And so he married a fancy woman with fancy airs and two fancy daughters with very persnickety ways of their own.

Everyone agreed that they were three awful women altogether.

And everyone agreed that it was awful indeed the way they treated the Buachaill Bó Beag.

The sisters called him Bó-Bó Big Foot and the stepmother put him out into the fields like a common cowherd, and him the son of the king of Ireland. The only one who did not mind was Bó Beag himself. He liked the windy hills and the fresh air and the constant company of Corcaigh the Bull. In fact, he was so cheerful and so beloved of the people of his tribe, that he managed to irritate the new queen even more than before, until at last she decided that both he and his bull had to go.

So, she visited the Dark Woman, the Bain Dubh, who lived under the trees in the deep part of the forest.

"What will you give me," the Bain Dubh whispered, "if I rid you of this troublesome boy and his bull?"

They whispered together of the price the new queen was willing to pay. "I need two girls to train up in the dark ways," said the Bain Dubh and when the new queen had agreed to that awful price, the Bain Dubh gave the stepmother a potion and told her to drink it.

"It will make you pale and tired," she whispered in her low, throaty voice, "and when you have taken to your bed, tell the king, your husband, that the only thing that will make you well again is to drink the blood of the Bó Beag's bull.

So, the queen took to her bed and called her husband to her and said that the only thing that would make her well was to kill the bull.

"No!" cried the king. "I cannot! For I promised the mother of the boy that I would keep them together forever."

But the stepmother grew more pale and more tired and when she called him to her again, the king was frightened by her pallor.

"Well," he said at last, "it is just a bull, and you are my wife."

Outside the door of the chamber, those who were listening told the Buachaill Bó Beag, who told the bull Corcaigh that the king had decided to kill him.

"No fear," said the Great Bull to Bó Beag. "But on the day of sacrifice, do all that I say."

The day came and the Buachaill Bó Beag led Corcaigh the Bull into the center of the rath with tears in his eyes.

But just before the warriors were sent forward with their knives, the bull called to Buachaill Bó Beag, "Jump on my back and hold fast to my horns."

Bó Beag did exactly that, and the great beast leaped into the air, striking the wan queen with his hooves before he cleared the stone wall of the rath, and came to rest in the fields far below, with Bó Beag clinging to his horns. Behind them, the crowd roared at the death of the stepmother, though whether the roar was one of joy or sorrow was never clear a t'all.

And Bó Beag and Corcaigh thundered away across Eire, out to the sea cliffs and over the high hills until at last they found an empty green field where they came to a stop, hungry and tired.

"We need a feast," said Corcaigh.

"There's plenty of grass for you, old friend," said Bó Beag, "though I think that I will be hungry a while longer."

"That's where you're wrong," said Corcaigh, "for I have magic in my left ear."

And sure enough, when Bó Beag reached into the great bull's ear, he withdrew a fine linen tablecloth. No sooner had he spread it on the ground than it was covered with fine ham and boiled potatoes, buttery biscuits and sweet honey cakes, and Bó Beag ate until he could hold no more. Then he shook it out again and it provided a blanket and a pillow for the Bó Beag to sleep.

By now it was nearly dusk, and they were a full and sleepy pair indeed, but just when Bó Beag had curled into Corcaigh's side and was drifting into dreams, they heard a deep bellow from the forest at the edge of the field.

The Buachaill Bó Beag sat up, wide awake.

"Now what do you suppose that is?" he asked Corcaigh.

Corcaigh gave him a strange answer. "You know that I am magic," he said.

"Of course I know," said the Buachaill Bó Beag. "What other bull could speak and fly and pull great feasts from his own left ear?"

"That one can," said Corcaigh.

"That bellowing one?"

"Just that one. This is his magical field, and I am on it."

"What will we do?" asked Bó Beag, but Corcaigh had already stood and lowered his head.

"I will fight him of course," said Corcaigh. "No fear now lad."

And then the great bull charged from the forest, its bellow louder than anything Bó Beag had ever heard because it had three heads. Still, he was no match for the magic Corcaigh, who defeated him soundly and slept more soundly still.

In the morning, they were awakened by a bellowing more terrible than before.

"I was afraid of this," said Corcaigh. "This will be the father of the one I defeated."

And sure enough it was, a bull with six great heads and a bellow that could be heard out to sea.

But Corcaigh defeated him handily, then bid Bó Beag to draw out the linen cloth and the two of them had a feast for a king and a good long nap in the spring sunshine.

Near dusk, there was a bellowing so fierce that the ground beneath them shook.

"Alas," said Corcaigh, "this is the grandfather come for me,"

"Well," said Bó Beag, "no fear. You'll defeat this one as well."

"No fear at all," said Corcaigh, "but I have gifts to give you. The napkin, of course, is yours, for I would never want you to be hungry or cold. Now reach into my right ear."

Bó Beag did as he was told and there withdrew a long stick, covered with twined carvings of birds and fish and leaping deer.

"Swing it around your head three times," Corcaigh commanded.

Bó Beag did as he was told. The great stick whistled around his head and then began to whine and then to sing. When Bó Beag looked up, in his hand was a great silver sword, shimmering with light, covered with carvings of birds and fish and leaping deer, and on its hilt, the figure of a great, horned bull.

"And now the last," said Corcaigh. "For when I am gone, you will take my tail and wear it as your belt, and it will protect you always."

"That will be when I'm old and gray," said Bó.

"Not so," said Corcaigh, "for this one will defeat me. But my gifts are always with you. And the love of my great heart."

And before Bó Beag could protest, a great magical bull with twelve heads came charging from the forest and locked horns with Corcaigh. The battle raged for three days and three nights, but when it was ended, Corcaigh lay dead on the field. The twelve-headed bull turned its baleful eyes toward Bó Beag, but he swung his walking stick three times around his head and killed the bull with a single swipe of the silver sword. Then the Buachaill Bó Beag leaned against the still form of Corcaigh and cried for three days and three nights until he was empty of tears.

Then he did as Corcaigh had told him to do, tied the tail around his waist and wandered down the hill to the hut of the *boaire,* the cattle man, and knocked on his door.

The *boaire* took one look at the short boy in the big boots, with the queer walking stick, the cowtail belt, and the cloak that looked like a tablecloth and hired him on the spot to herd his cows.

And so in secret and in sorrow, the lonely son of the king of Corc became a cowherd.

Three years passed without incident, but then one day when Bó Beag was in the field with his cattle, he heard a thundering voice, "Are you the one who slew my bull?" it cried. "For I see you wear the tail."

"He was my brother," Bó Beag answered and even as he said so, a three-headed giant launched himself from the forest toward the little cattle boy. But Bó swung the stick with its strange markings three times around his head and whistled off the head of that giant before he had even stopped spinning.

And so it went for three days in a row as the three-headed giant was followed by the six-headed companion and then the twelve.

And when those days were finished, the Buachaill Bó Beag had become a warrior and was ready to venture into the wide green world.

That very day, the *boaire* returned from the market with a strange story indeed.

"Hear this," he said to Bó Beag, who had become like a son to him. "A giant sea-dragon has been burning down the palace of the king every year, and the people have decided to use their young princess as bait to catch the dragon. They say she's not much to look at, a little plain, with curly hair that frizzes in the rain. And stubborn as a bull. But still. To tie her up as dragon meat? They say that champions from far and wide competed for the chance to defend her. I, for one, plan to go back to the rath to see the spectacle."

"Not I," said the Buachaill Bó Beag. "For I have cattle to mind."

But all night long he couldn't stop thinking about the frizzy-haired girl who was stubborn as a bull. He decided that he didn't think much of a tuath who would offer their dear one to a dragon. So when the *boaire* left for the rath of the king, Bó Beag followed him.

From the cliff above the sea, he watched as they fastened the waist of the princess to a great rock. He was unimpressed with her first champion, a golden-haired handsome young man who wandered back and forth along the beach swinging his sword in the air and smoothing his braided hair. He was even less impressed when the mincing prince ran away as soon as the great green dragon began to lift its head from the sea.

"Don't leave me!" cried the princess. "You skinny bag of bones! At least throw me your sword so that I stand a fighting chance!"

But the champion had vanished, and the great green dragon lowered its long scaly head toward the helpless girl.

Just then, from the headland above the beach, came the whipping sound of a bull-belt lasso. Riding it down to the dragon's back was a wild red-headed boy with huge, booted feet and a cloak that looked like a tablecloth. He swung onto the back of the dragon, and when the great beast tried to dislodge him, he laughed aloud with delight.

"I've ridden Corcaigh, the Great Bull of Corc! Do ye think ye're any match for me?"

Then he swung his strange stick over his head three times and plunged a silver sword into the eye of the dragon.

With a howl, the dragon swooped down toward the princess, but the Buachaill Bó Beag simply used the ride to cut her loose.

"Hello there darlin' girl," he said as he swooped by. "Fancy meeting you here." The princess laughed aloud.

The dragon reared up into the air, spewing fire and howling in pain. In a swift arc, it plunged toward the sea, throwing the Buachaill Bó Beag high into the air. He held tight to his sword and his bull tail lasso, but as Bó Beag flew toward the high cliffs, one of his boots flew off and landed in the sand below. The princess rushed to scoop it up.

At the top of the cliff, the Buachaill Bó Beag tied his bull belt around his waist, shook his sword back into stick form, and on one booted foot, limped back to his cattle fields.

But the princess knew that she had met her match. Funny and fearless, stubborn and quirky, she had fallen in love with the big footed boy who owned the boot. When her father and all the tuath protested that no one knew him, or that he was not a handsome boy at all, she answered simply, "He saved my life and made me laugh all at the same time. I will marry no one but the man whose foot will fit this boot."

She announced throughout the land that she would hold a great *feis* with feasting and racing and dancing and that she would try the boot on the foot of every man in the kingdom.

Now the Buachaill Bó Beag had not been able to stop thinking about the princess who had laughed aloud while she was tied to a rock and face to face with a fire-breathing dragon.

So off he went to the *feis*, barefoot and dressed in his cattle clothes, his bull-tail belt tied around his waist, in his cloak that looked like a tablecloth, leaning on his odd stick with its twined carvings.

At the great rath of the king, he stood in line with all the princes in their fancy cloaks and tunics and said nothing at all when they hooted that no princess "would ever marry a barefooted cattle boy in a tablecloth."

When he came to the head of the line, he put out his great foot, the one and only foot that fit the boot.

On the dais high above him, the princess laughed aloud. "Hello darlin' boy," she called. "Fancy meeting you here."

"Fancy indeed," said the Buachaill Bó Beag, and the two of them laughed at their own joke.

"You cannot marry a cattle boy," the king protested.

"Cattle boy or king, I can and will," said the princess. "For he saved my life and made me laugh aloud."

"He is the ugliest boy I have ever seen," said the king. "Why would you ever marry such a one?"

At this, the princess's eyes grew wide.

"Ugly?" she said. "Look again, father. For surely, here is the handsomest warrior in all of Ireland."

At her words, the Buachaill Bó Beag shook out his tablecloth cloak. Not only did it spread a feast between them, but it dressed him in the seven colors of a king. He swung his great stick in the air, and when his carved silver sword was in his hand, he called aloud,

"I am the son of the king of Corc and the brother of Corcaigh the magical bull."

"No matter," said the princess. "King or cattle boy, you are mine."

And so, just so, they were married, and they took care of each other and made each other laugh for all the years of their long and happy life together.

Is fírinne sin.

This is the truth of the telling.

Chapter 6

Original Folktale

This is an original folktale, and I offer it here to anyone who has lost someone they love. In other words, I offer it to all of ye. I dedicate it to my dear departed friend, teacher, thesis advisor, Father Andrew Greeley, who once told me "The God in whom we believe restores all things." I choose to hope in that. I hope that you can too.

Maura O'Meara and the Wellstone

Maura O'Meara's mother was sick. She had been sick the whole of the long, wet winter. Each morning, Maura O'Meara made her mother a cup of hot tea; each day her mother seemed to grow a little weaker, coughing under the mounds of quilts that Maura O'Meara had piled on her. Came the day when Maither could not even raise her head to drink her tea.

So, Maura O'Meara put on her best wool dress and the soft green cloak that Maither had made her. She brushed her hair until it shone, hung her mother's basket over her arm, and started out her door along the road beside the sea.

Nosy Nellie Mac Fergus came running up beside her.

"Is your mother better today, Maura O'Meara?"

"She is not, I thank you for asking."

"Then where are you going if she is feeling poorly?"

"I am going to see Old Meg, the witch woman."

227

Nosy Nellie gasped. "You can't go there. Old Meg puts spells on little girls. She sells them to the Other People. Sometimes she eats them for lunch."

"If she can help my mother, I'll gladly go live with the Others." Maura O'Meara rounded a bend in the road where Old Meg's cottage came into view. She took a deep breath. "And besides, I am too skinny for lunch."

Nellie stopped running beside Maura. She raised her pudgy hands and stared at them for a moment.

"I'm going home," she called and started back for the village.

Maura O'Meara did not even turn to look at her. She had made up her mind. Everyone knew that when Maura O'Meara made up her mind, nothing would stop her at all, at all. She marched directly to the door of Old Meg's cottage. For a moment she glanced around her, then she raised her hand and knocked hard on the wood of the door.

"Come in," cawed a raspy, witchlike voice. Maura's hand trembled, but she opened the door. The little cottage was much neater than Maura O'Meara would have expected from a witch. Tied bundles of roots and flowers hung in bunches from the rafters. The furniture was neatly patched, and the cottage smelled like warm honey.

A beady-eyed black bird perched on the middle of the little table, pecking at crumbs. He turned and looked at Maura O'Meara.

"Come in," he said again, in his raspy voice.

Maura O'Meara laughed aloud. Suddenly the bird lifted and flew at her! Maura ducked her head beneath her arms and whirled around to run. There in the doorway was Old Meg, the bird perched on her wrist. Her hair was long and grey, twisted in a braid at the back of her head. Sprigs of what looked like leaves and twigs were caught in it. A basket that hung from her elbow was full of flowers and roots and the stems of plants dangling at odd angles from the edges. Old Meg's dress seemed to be made of patches of every color—the blue of the sea, the green of the stones at the shore, the red of blood. She stared at Maura O'Meara.

"What are you doing here?" she asked in an angry voice.

Maura O'Meara raised up her stubborn little chin and held her knees together to stop them from trembling.

"My mother is sick, and I came here for you to heal her."

"Go to the doctor in the village."

"I went to him all winter. He gave me medicines and I used them all. My mother is still no better."

"And where do you think he gets all of his fine medicines?"

Maura O'Meara looked again at the bundles of dried things hanging from the ceiling.

"So, you really are a healer?"

"I am. Now, go away. I can't help your mother."

Maura O'Meara's shoulders sagged. She hung her head and started toward the door. At the doorway, she turned back.

"Why do they even bother to call you a witch? What good are you, if you can't help my mother?"

Old Meg looked surprised, but she gave an answer.

"They call me a witch because long ago, I had some visits with the banshee. Do you know who the banshee is, little girl?"

"Everyone knows that," said Maura. "She's one of the Other People. She sings at the window when someone is going to die."

"She does that," said the old woman, nodding. "But that is not all she does. Great fools." She waved her arm toward the village. "They are afraid of me because the banshee visited me. They are afraid I will bring them bad luck, so they call me a witch and they all stay away. And now you should go away too." She flapped her arms to push Maura O'Meara out onto the stoop, then shut the door right in the little girl's face.

That night Maura O'Meara made her mother hot tea with sugar. She propped pillows as high behind her mother's back as she could get them and spooned the tea into her mother's lips, dabbing up the spilled drops.

"You must have some, Maither," she whispered. "The tea will help you to get strong."

Maither managed a small smile and patted Maura's hand.

"Strong," she whispered. But she could not sip any more tea. She leaned her head back against the pillows and closed her eyes.

Maura O'Meara watched her for a moment, then raised her stubborn chin. She fastened her soft green cloak around her again, took the lantern from the peg by the door, and marched out into the darkness. When she reached Old Meg's door, she pounded with her fists until the witch opened the door. Old Meg was dressed in a soft woolen nightgown, the grey braid twisting over her shoulder. She looked like somebody's grandmother in the yellow lantern light.

"Tell me where to find the banshee," Maura O'Meara demanded.

"You can't just go off and find the banshee, silly girl. The banshee has to find you."

"Then where did the banshee find you?"

For a moment, the old woman's face looked so sad that Maura O'Meara thought she might cry.

"She found me wandering by the sea in the light of a full winter moon."

"Then I will go by the sea and wait. I will wait there every night until the full moon and past, if I have to."

Maura O'Meara turned to go.

"Wait a minute child." The old woman put out a wrinkled hand. "You can't just go and find the banshee. The banshee will require a trade. She sings the end of a life. You are just a little girl."

"I know this," said Maura O'Meara. "I am prepared to trade. I will go to live with her, with the Other People. That is what I will trade for my mother's life."

Now the old woman knelt down and looked hard into the face of Maura O'Meara.

"So," she muttered, "You have come after all."

Maura O'Meara looked behind her into the darkness.

"Who has come?" she asked, confused.

But Old Meg just shook her head.

"Come in. There is something I must show you."

Inside the cottage, the old woman unwrapped a parcel, hidden beneath layers of soft wool. She set it on the table before Maura O'Meara. It was a speckled oval stone, green as the sea, blue as a sunlit wave. Little lights seemed to sparkle deep within it. Maura O'Meara gasped at its beauty.

"What is it?"

"The banshee gave it to me. I was weeping by the sea, and she came to comfort me. She was gentle and beautiful. She said it was a wellstone. I asked her what good to me was a stone from an old well, but she said that someone would come who would make me understand. I never believed that until today."

The old woman was already hurrying to the clothing pegs beside her bed.

"You bring the lantern, child. And there on the bench, my basket of simples. I must put on my dress and cloak so we can go to see your mother."

At Maura O'Meara's cottage, the old woman felt the forehead of Maura's mother. She lifted her arms and placed her fingers on the wrist. She bent her head and listened to the raspy breathing. Then she stood.

"As bad as you said and worse, child. But I will do what I can."

And so, Old Meg the witch moved in with Maura O'Meara and her mother.

For many days Old Meg nursed Maura's mother. She made her teas of herbs, spread boiled leeks against her chest, bathed her, and steamed her but nothing seemed to bring her about.

Of course, the village was shocked; everyone avoided the O'Meara cottage.

"Old Meg will bring the banshee!" nosy Nellie Mac Fergus called from the road before the cottage, afraid to come any closer.

But Maura O'Meara paid no mind.

She simply stayed by her mother's side. She did not run off with the other children, even when the warm winds turned April to May. She boiled herbs in the kettle and fluffed pillows and made tea. Old Meg watched her always, saying nothing. But late one night when the little girl was very tired, Old Meg gathered Maura O'Meara onto her lap and sang the old songs, rocking gently until the little girl slept in her arms. And that was the night that Old Meg remembered how to smile.

And then one evening, Maura O'Meara's mother seemed to wake. She looked up to see Old Meg bending over her and she said a surprising thing.

"How sad for you, Meg, after your own beautiful girl. But now you must take my Maura as your own, for I will be leaving." She closed her eyes at the effort of speaking.

"What does she mean?" asked Maura from the opposite side of the bed. "What about your own girl? Why will you take me as your own?"

"Never mind," said Meg. "Come here and fluff these pillows, child."

"No," said Maura O'Meara, raising her stubborn chin. "Tell me about your own little girl. Tell me why you were crying by the sea. Meg, I cannot bear it if my mother leaves."

Old Meg turned her face to the firelight.

"Many years ago, I could not bear it either. Many years ago, when my own little girl was called by the banshee. When she left, all the love went out of my life."

"But I love you, of course," said Maura O'Meara.

For a moment, Old Meg looked surprised. She cupped her hand under Maura O'Meara's chin and suddenly she laughed aloud. It was the first time Maura O'Meara had heard her laugh.

"Of course!" cried Old Meg. "Of course!" She walked to the window and called out into the dark night. "I understand, woman of the Shee."

"Understand what?" cried Maura O'Meara, afraid, but Meg had already thrown on her cloak and opened the door to the night. In the doorway, she knelt and opened her arms to Maura O'Meara, who ran to her and hugged her hard around the neck.

"Don't leave us," she whispered.

"I will always be with you Maura O'Meara. Always. And I promise that your mother will not leave you now." She hugged the little girl hard, then stood.

"Shut the door and draw the curtains," Old Meg said briskly. "You will hear singing, but you must not open the door until morning. Just hold your mother's hand and be still tonight."

And then she was gone.

The breeze whispered in and lifted a curl of Maura's hair.

All night long, Maura heard the singing, strange and beautiful and sad. For a time, it was close to the window, soft and plaintive, like a dove. Later, it reminded Maura of the wind just before a storm. Just before dawn, the singing moved away, along the curved road by the sea. It lingered there, deep and sonorous like whale songs. At last, when the morning light misted around the edges of the door and the eerie singing of the night ceased, Maura O'Meara shook herself up from the chair by her mother's side. She moved wearily to the kettle and boiled up her mother's tea. She put in some sugar and brought a spoon from the drawer, ready to ladle the tea into her mother's mouth. But when she turned back to the bed, her mother was sitting up, with the pillows propped behind her!

"Maither!" cried Maura O'Meara as she ran into the outstretched arms.

"How good it is to hold you," said her mother. "I feel so much better today, but I had the strangest dream that I was being nursed by Old Meg, the witch woman. I even thought I heard her singing." Maura's mother laughed. "But you were my nurse. My little light!" And she hugged Maura O'Meara even tighter.

"But Old Meg *was* here, Maither," cried Maura. "Winter has turned to spring, and she stayed with us all the while. I must go and tell her now that you are well!"

Maura O'Meara's feet flew along the road that curved by the sea, lifted like gull's wings on the joy of her mother's recovery.

"Is your Maither well?" cried nosy Nellie Mac Fergus from behind her cottage wall.

"She is well!" cried Maura O'Meara. "She is well because Old Meg nursed her. Tell that to the village."

The people, hearing, began to follow Maura down the road. They gathered in a cluster behind her, murmuring that perhaps they had been wrong about Meg all along.

"Meg!" Maura O'Meara cried joyously from the roadway, "Meg!" At the door there was no answer, but it creaked open gently in the warm May breeze. Old Meg was nowhere to be found, nor was she ever seen again.

But shimmering in the sunlight on the table was the wellstone. Beneath it was a note, in a joyful scrawl.

"For my beloved Maura O'Meara," it read. *"All will be well. Oh yes, all will be well."*

Folktales

Whooo wants to know more?

What Is Folklore?

Folktales are very different from both myths and legends.

Folklore is, in some ways, a diminution. It shrinks or stretches vast mythic peoples and heroes. It turns them into fairies and giants. Irish folktales specifically turn the great god Lugh Samildánach into a leprechaun and the great hero Fionn Mac Cumhaill into a thumb-sucking giant.

Why do they do this? Likely, the coming of Christianity has a great deal to do with this shapeshifting of older stories. Tales of pagan gods might no longer be acceptable fare, so the magical Tuatha de Danaan shrink and become fairy folk, not deities in any way, but still present in the reductive stories. They are no longer the *sidhe*—the Others—with their dangerous, long-lived powers. They are *sidheóg*—the good people, the fair folk, the fairy folk. Now, they dance under the hawthorn bushes throughout Ireland, playing on their harps and fiddles. Likewise, Fionn Mac Cumhaill, in becoming a somewhat silly giant, is no longer a legendary warrior. He is just a big galumphing man at the center of exaggerated tales.

Another factor in folktales is landscape and the natural world around us. My teacher, Abenaki storyteller and writer Joseph Bruchac, tells a wonderful tale about how the chipmunk got a striped tail (he managed to irritate a large, sleepy bear). Finn serves a similar function when he becomes a giant. How *do* we explain the Giant's Causeway in the far north of Ireland? Doesn't it make sense that giants once walked on it between Ireland and Scotland? So, a folktale arises.

Consider all of the things that cannot be explained. Ghostly lights that move above the bog. The sad human eyes of the seals, the sounds like singing inside a watery cave. For example, here in America, thunder in the Catskill Mountains became little men who played at ninepins and put Rip Van Winkle to sleep for twenty years. How do we explain how thunder magnifies and repeats in a narrow mountain pass? How do we explain a bone-lazy man who does nothing? Folktales can explain all of these.

Folk and fairy tales also operate as cautionary tales. They teach children what and what not to do. They model what constitutes wit and what constitutes stupidity. So, if a man gets drunk, wanders around in the darkness, and falls into a bog, the story might result in high hilarity, but with a whiptail. This will get you lost. This will get you drowned. This will get you laughed at.

Scary stories often function this way. Make no mistake, folk and fairy tales can be downright grisly. For example, a famous Irish folktale challenges young men to go and find out why a folk character called the *gruach gaire* (a laughing, hairy goblin) is no longer laughing. Sounds like a lighthearted tale, right? And yet, for each young man who does not solve the question, the result is horrific. The king cuts off their heads and posts them on a pike by his castle door. Shades of *Game of Thrones!*

Folktales are fireside tales. They serve as bridges between times, between cultures, between the natural world and the human world, between adults and children, between light and darkness. For us, as Americans, think of them as tales we would tell by a campfire, marshmallows on skewers, ready to melt a s'more.

Sources for Irish Folklore

Croker, Thomas Crofton. *Fairy Legends and Traditions of the South of Ireland* (Legare Street Press, 2021). Originally published in 1824.

Curtin, Jeremiah. *Myths and Folklore of Ireland* (Wings Books, 1996). Originally published in 1889.

Glassie, Henry, ed. *Irish Folk Tales* (Pantheon Books, 1985).

Hyde, Douglas & Alfred Turner Nutt. *Beside the Fire: A Collection of Irish Gaelic Folk Stories.* (Legare Street Press, 2022). Originally published in 1890.

Jacobs, Joseph. *Celtic Fairy Tales* (Dover, 1968). Originally published by David Nutt, in 1892.

Wilde, Lady Francesca Speranza. *Legends, Charms and Superstitions of Ireland* (Dover Publications 2006). Originally published in 1887.

Yeats, W.B., ed. *Fairy and Folk Tales of Ireland* (Macmillan, 1973 ed). Originally published in 1888.

Methods for Collecting and Telling Folktales

True folklorists are scribes. They travel among the people of the villages and the rural areas. They sit by their fires. They listen. Before voice recorders, they scribbled down everything they heard. Nowadays, they often tape and then transcribe. Nowadays, you can often listen to the original teller as he spins his story. When a good folklorist gets a story down, that story is in the exact voice of the teller, so it has idioms, colloquialisms, the speech patterns of the teller and even the interruptions when the teller relights his pipe or talks about someone in the village. Written transcription might sometimes be difficult to understand because of those language quirks, but it is always a delight, because in addition to reading the story in its own place and in its own vernacular, the reader has the added pleasure of picking up the character of the teller, his sense of humor perhaps, or his worldview. This kind of transcription work is what you would find in the sources above.

A second method is contextualized telling. The transcription is still present, but the folklorist now sets the scene. He might tell you what the little cabin looks like or try to capture the smell of the peat fire. He might give you a description of your teller as a wizened old man with a white beard and a crackling laugh and a tendency to smoke one pipe after another. In this type of folklore, the folklorist is trying to bring you into the setting in which the story was originally told, as well as let you meet the original teller.

A third method is a retelling. That is what you are reading in this book. I have spent my entire teaching life bringing my students into Irish history and literature through retellings. Retellings will keep the core of the story, but they may change language to make it more comprehensible to a modern reader or to remove idioms and colloquialisms that modern people no longer know. Retellings may change pacing. Often, also, retellings will use more action, dialogue, and conflict with less narrator intrusion and sometimes less description. Retellings are written with their readers in mind; how do these readers differ from the original listeners and readers of this story?

The final method is oral telling. Oral storytelling has a kind of intrinsic magic. Breton storytellers often begin their stories with the incantation *Once upon a time when there was no time.* I tend to begin many of my tellings with *Fado, fado, long, long ago.* Oral storytellings will transport the listener out of the room, out of their time. I first discovered this magic when I was tasked with teaching *Macbeth* to eighth grade students in Little Appalachia. Really? Macbeth? For eighth grade? So, I decided to bring them into ancient Scotland with oral storytelling. At first, they were their usual squirmy selves, despite my costume, but then the voice that came out of me was not my voice, and the mood in the room changed. They leaned forward in their chairs and their jaws dropped open. They were absorbing the story, vanishing into the story, allowing the story to surround them. I like to think that they were swallowing the story, that it was feeding a deep human hunger. From that day forward, they asked for Macbeth every single day. When you watch a good teller, watch for their tools and tricks. Phrases will repeat. Stories may contain musical interludes or poems or rhymes. Voices will change. Body language will pull you in or push you away. Numbers will repeat and will be magical. In Celtic stories, in particular, things will often repeat in threes. Pauses will be carefully orchestrated to bring home the delivery line that will cause the audience to laugh, or gasp, or weep. The end result is a shared human experience that can never be exactly duplicated again.

Index